ROCHESTER FROM THE WEST

The year 1989 marks the bicentennial of manufacturing in Rochester beginning with the founding of Ebenezer (Indian) Allan's Mills. Through cooperation between industry and community, Rochester has grown to be a major technologically based manufacturing area. It is in recognition of this bicentennial and with appreciation to the community that the Industrial Management Council presents this book to the citizens of Rochester.

What more appropriate organization should benefit from the sale of this book than the Friends of the Rochester Public Library. Their service to the community includes programs such as the Rochester Literary Award which recognizes outstanding living American authors. The sale of this book will help to establish an endowment fund for this award.

MANUFACTURING BICENTENNIAL
Rochester, New York
1 7 8 9 - 1 9 8 9

ROCHESTER
A PICTORIAL HISTORY

by Ruth Rosenberg-Naparsteck
City Historian of Rochester, New York

THE
DONNING COMPANY
PUBLISHERS
NORFOLK/VIRGINIA BEACH

This book is dedicated
to my husband, Martin and to my
children, Taft, America, and Molly-Maguire.

The Donning Company/Publishers
5659 Virginia Beach Boulevard
Norfolk, Virginia 23502

Edited by Elizabeth B. Bobbitt
Richard A. Horwege, Senior Editor
Designed by Joan Croyder

Library of Congress Cataloging-in-Publication Data:

Rosenberg-Naparsteck, Ruth, 1950-
 Rochester: a pictorial history / by Ruth Rosenberg-
Naparsteck. p. cm.
  Includes bibliographical references.
  ISBN 0-89865-783-0
  1. Rochester (N.Y.)—History—Pictorial works.
2. Rochester (N.Y.)—Description—Views.
I. Title.
F129.R743R67   1989
974.7'89—dc20   89-37456
                                 CIP

Printed in the United States of America

CONTENTS

An unidentified man takes a drink from a fountain at a fire hydrant in the 1920s. From the City Bureau of Public Information

PREFACE

Rochester, the photographic capital of America, with its long-established industrial production in that field, its notable museum of photography, and now its unique photographic archives, well merits the pictorial portrayal of its history that Ruth Rosenberg-Naparsteck has compiled. As City Historian she has assembled an unprecedented profusion of pictorial views of Rochester scenes and personalities ranging from its Indian predecessors through its early pioneer and boom-town days, its successive Flour City and Flower City periods, and its more recent industrial and metropolitan eras. She has cast a wide net, capturing ethnic, religious and social, as well as economic and architectural features of the city's life and development, and she has supplied informative captions that help to place each view in its historic setting.

Her accompanying text, which ties ten successive pictorial chapters together in historical relationships, has an episodic quality that will stir the reminiscences of older residents and spark the curiosity of recent newcomers. By diligent search through many picture files Ruth Rosenberg-Naparsteck has unearthed and included many views never before reproduced and her book will open fascinating new vistas for many Rochesterians.

Blake McKelvey
City Historian Emeritus

ACKNOWLEDGMENTS

Without the insights and recollections of many people, no historian can write the history of a city. I found people to be anxious to lend their help and they were especially interested in the photographs they had not seen before. Photographs are a part of our history that is still not used to its greatest potential. I thank the many people who helped to collect the photographs, many previously unpublished, that make this illustrated history strong.

The Local History Division at the Rochester Public Library was very helpful in pointing out diaries and letters as well as photographs. Linda Bretz, director of the Library, has been supportive and encouraging in this project.

Karl Kabelac, librarian at Rush Rhees Library at the University of Rochester helped by pointing out little known resources. Robert Gullo, director of Lavery Library at St. John Fisher, gave me information on numerous occasions and shared with me the library's large collection of postcards and photographs. Lea Kemp, the librarian at the Rochester Museum and Science Center, offered many suggestions for resources.

Without the cooperation of Gannett Newspapers, many of the photographs that record our city's history would not be available to the public in this book. The photographs in their collection record some of our most significant historical events and many have not been published since they first appeared in the newspaper.

I also wish to thank the International Museum of Photography at George Eastman House for making available the Charles Zoller Collection of previously unpublished photographs. My special thanks to Mark Hager for printing the photographs and sharing his knowledge of them. These photographs illuminate scenes of everyday life in the city in the early decades of the century. Rochester is indeed fortunate to remain the home of this museum.

I also thank Jean Ingham of the National Technical Institute for the Deaf at the Rochester Institute of Technology and Mrs. Pat Zwick of the Rochester School for the Deaf for sharing information and photographs on the history of the education of the deaf, a little published aspect of our city's history.

Many people shared their insights and recollections with me, including Joseph Caccamise, Ed Spelman, Hans Munsch, and George West. Peter Jemison, seventh generation grandson of Mary Jemison, the "white woman of the Genesee," gave me a tour of Gannondagan, the site of the Seneca village in Victor destroyed by the Marquis de Denonville. Standing on these unspoiled grounds closed the centuries and allowed me as a historian to get a sense of the once large Seneca village and its people.

Anne Corcoran and Tim O'Connel were very helpful with information about maps and photographs throughout the city. Ira Srole, the City photographer, pointed out many photographs necessary for other projects that eventually became a part of this book. Bill Davis shared his years of research on the river and its early settlements as well as a photograph of the Port of Rochester in 1856 originally published in *Frank Leslie's Illustrated Weekly*. Thomas X. Grasso, president of the Canal Society of Western New York, shared his knowledge of the canal and its effect on Rochester's history as well as his drawings of boatyards

and mills. I also thank the staffs of the Baden
Street Settlement House and the Lewis Street
Settlement House for consulting with me on the
development of their neighborhood's history.

Joan Sullivan read early drafts of parts of this
book and pointed out research or illustrations she
came across in her own research. Cindy Glaze, Ed
Spelman, and Bonnie Deisenroth shared family
photographs that make this book a history of the
people of the city. The Rochester Historical Society preserved many of the photographs that
appear in this book. Without their diligence and
hours of volunteer work, much of our city's
history would be lost.

I thank my husband for his patience while I
spent more than a year on the research and writ-
ing of this book. My special thanks goes to Dr.
Blake McKelvey, City Historian Emeritus and
Historian Shirley Cox-Husted for their reading
and rereading of this manuscript in its many
drafts. Their criticisms were critical to the final
form of this book, however, I must be responsible
for any errors.

Ruth Rosenberg-Naparsteck
City Historian

*The Children's Pavilion was once filled
with people enjoying band music and the
sights of Highland Park. The Pavilion
was dedicated to the children of Rochester by the Ellwanger and Barry Nursery
in 1888, the year the nursery gave the
land that formed the nucleus of the Rochester Parks System. On this beautiful
summer day around the turn of the century, a carriage draws people through the
park harnessed to a dapple-gray horse.
From the Rochester Public Library*

Chapter One

French explorers, missionaries, and priests made contact with the Iroquois as early as 1535 when Jacques Cartier sailed up the St. Lawrence River. Explorers mapped the Genesee River and the Great Lakes. Etienne Brule, the first white man to cross the Genesee River, traveled with Cartier. La Salle paddled into the Irondequoit Bay, stopping at Indian Landing. Competition for the fur trade among the Senecas, the French, and the English, led to the march of Canada's governor, Marquis de Denonville, on the Seneca villages in 1687.
From the Rochester Historical Society collection at the Rochester Public Library

FROM A SENECA HUNTING GROUND TO A SETTLERS' HOMESTEAD:
The Wilderness of the Genesee Country

THE SENECA INDIANS

The Seneca Indians, strongest of the Iroquois tribes, lived in multi-family bark longhouses in small villages scattered about the Finger Lakes. They were farmers and hunters who traded extensively with other villages. Hunters built temporary shelters from bark and hides stretched over frames that looked to many pioneers like wigwams. They were built along the river and the creeks at the fording places like King's Landing at the Lower Falls and near the present Court Street Bridge, Charlotte, Maplewood Park, Seneca Park, Genesee Valley Park, and near the University of Rochester.

The swampy, rattlesnake infested Genesee River valley did not attract Seneca settlement. But Indian hunting parties traveled the numerous paths to the lake and bay shores and crossed the Genesee River near the present Court Street, or at another crossing just north of the Lower Falls. Indian shelters were set up along the shores and by springs near St. Luke's Church and about Corn Hill. The wilderness area on which Rochester now stands was once so abundant with fish and wildlife that pioneers reported taking hundreds of squirrels and rattlesnakes and scores of beaver and deer in one day. Barrels of salmon and other fish could be caught at the Lower Falls. Bears and wolves roamed the wilderness.

Indians traded furs at the French trading post at Fort des Sables near present Seabreeze as early as 1716 and at the British Fort Schuyler at Indian Landing on the bay as early as 1721 where Peter Schuyler opened his trading post. The Iroquois enjoyed a self-sufficient economy before their trade with the French and the British made them dependent upon them.

The French and British fur speculators wanted as many furs as the Indians could provide. The Senecas eagerly traded furs for firearms, rum, kettles, and other supplies. Beaver skins in particular commanded a high price in Europe. The Senecas, keepers of the "western door" of the Iroquois Nation, became the principal suppliers of beaver pelts to both the French in Canada and the British.

But they overextended their territory when they tried to dominate the Upper Lakes and Canada. The Hurons and the Eries fought to push them out. Two thousand French and Indians marched on the Senecas in 1687 under Jacques Rene de Brisay, Marquis de Denonville, governor of Canada. All along Denonville's path from the landing on Irondequoit Bay, the army destroyed Iroquois villages and supplies. En route to Gannagaro (now Gannondagan, a State Historic Site) near Victor, the young Seneca braves fought Denonville's advancing army before retreating. Denonville hoped to capture them all in the fort, but when he found that all had escaped into the forest, he slaughtered their animals and burned their corn. The destruction of the animals and thousands of bushels of corn left the Indians begging for food and the women and children cowering in the forest, their homes reduced to smoldering ashes.

But the demand for furs was strong and the French and Indian trade soon resumed. The Indians quickly responded to British protests about trading with the French, by trading with the British, too, at Fort Schuyler. From both the French and the British, the Senecas accepted help from smiths, traders, and Roman Catholic missionaries. The priests, of course, influenced their culture, but the dependence on the French and the British for smiths and the desire for supplies from the traders destroyed the self-sufficiency that had once been the strength of the Iroquois Nation. This dependence led the Iroquois into an unfortunate political involvement in relations between the French and the British.

The increasing tensions between the French and the British caused irreversible damage to the once strong Iroquois Nation. The League that was once indivisible, once militarily unbeatable, was penetrated by trade; and the differing economic considerations of the tribes set the League back to the days when the tribes had squabbled among themselves.

Once again, the tribes became vulnerable. During the French and Indian War, many of the Senecas became mercenaries for one or the other battling armies. They were further decimated by exposure to smallpox and rum.

The alliance of the Iroquois Nation with the British during the American Revolution brought that nation to its knees when the British signed a peace treaty with the Americans that established the border of the United States across British held lands south of the Great Lakes. The United States signed a separate treaty with the now broken Iroquois Nation, recognizing their soil rights to the lands west of Cayuga Lake as Iroquois lands and requiring representation of United States officials in any land sales.

Some of the Senecas, their lifestyle having been influenced by their trade and dependence on Europeans, adopted the tools of the white man and began to build log homes. Most of them moved to the Upper Genesee Valley and the Niagara region. By the end of the Revolution, the wealth of the Iroquois in furs was exhausted, but the new traders, the settlers, were interested in something that the Iroquois had an abundance of—land. Unfortunately, despite the representation of the United States government at the treaty fires, the Iroquois were inadequately paid for their lands.

THE PHELPS AND GORHAM PURCHASE

The titles to the land that Oliver Phelps and Nathaniel Gorham and their associates wanted to buy were owned by both Massachusetts and the Iroquois Nation. Phelps purchased the rights to buy the land from Massachusetts in 1787 and in July of 1788, he and other investors left Massachusetts for the wilderness of western New York to purchase land from the Iroquois. Phelps and

Early pioneers recalled the Seneca Indian hunting wigwams located along the banks of the river and at the spring near St. Luke's Church in the present downtown Rochester. The wigwams were probably temporary hunting shelters and not as neatly built as these portrayed in A History of the City of Rochester *by John DeVoy, published by the* Post Express Printing Company.

his party met a representative of Massachusetts, the U.S. government, other speculators, and representatives of the Iroquois Nation at Buffalo Creek, then a sparsely settled wilderness.

The mood at the Council Fire was tense as Red Jacket, a respected chief of the Senecas, objected to the sale and recalled the atrocities and injustices inflicted on the Iroquois by the white men. Tense negotiations continued for two days before Farmer's Brother, the grand sachem, moderated the tone set by Red Jacket, thus allowing Phelps and other investors to successfuly negotiate the title to 2.6 million acres. The Iroquois set the Genesee River as the western border of the sale, but by offering the services of a sawmill and a gristmill, Phelps pursuaded the Indians to grant a tract of land on the west side of the river almost as large as the western half of the present Monroe County. Considering that an acre of land along the river was sufficient for a mill seat, Phelps had acquired a generous gift. For more than 2.6 million acres, Phelps paid twenty-one hundred

pounds in New York currency and promised five hundred pounds annually forever.

The Iroquois were angry when they learned a year after the sale of their land, that the New York pound was worth only half of its five dollar value in Canada. Though they accepted the final payment, they refused to sign an endorsement of final payment as a protest.

When Phelps had the land surveyed, an additional eighty-seven thousand acres were accidentally added to the tract. A protest by the Indians demanded another survey and a return of the disputed land that later became known as the Triangle because of the triangular shape of the tract between the straight northerly line of the western border drawn by the first surveyor and the corrected angular easterly line that was originally supposed to parallel the river. With the survey corrected, Phelps divided the land into six-mile square townships. In 1789 he opened a land office in Canandaigua, the first land office in America opened for the sale of wilderness land to settlers.

An Iroquois man and woman in typical dress from the frontispiece of the League of the Iroquois *by Lewis Henry Morgan, 1901.*

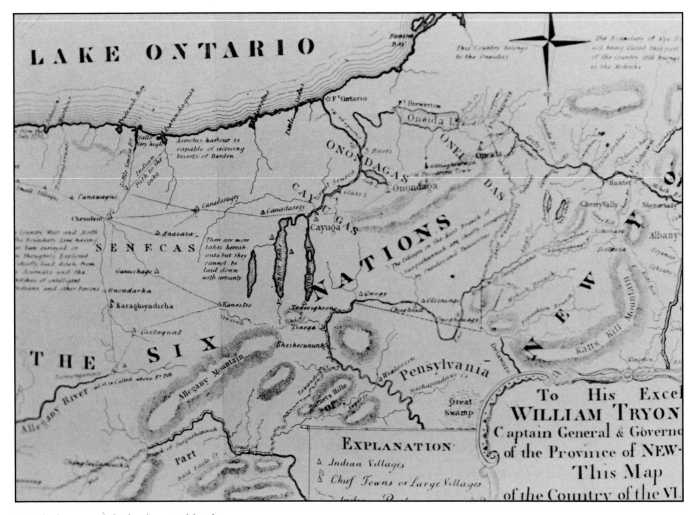

*Detail of a map of the lands owned by the
Six Nations of the Iroquois in 1771.
From an engraving in E. B. O'Callaghan's
Documentary History of the State of
New York, vol. 4, Albany, 1851;
from the Rochester Public Library*

*Red Jacket was a Seneca chief who objected
to the sale of Iroquois land at the council
fire at Buffalo Creek. He recalled the injustices and atrocities the Iroquois suffered
because of the whites. Historian Henry
O'Reilly wrote in 1838 that Oliver Phelps,
Nathaniel Gorham, and other land investors
were negotiating in a dangerous atmosphere
at the Council Fires because the Iroquois
were still angry about Gen. John Sullivan's
destructive march on their villages in 1779.
Farmer's Brother calmed the negotiations
and the sale of land was completed.
From W. L. Stone's Life and Times of Red
Jacket, Albany, 1866; from the Rochester
Public Library*

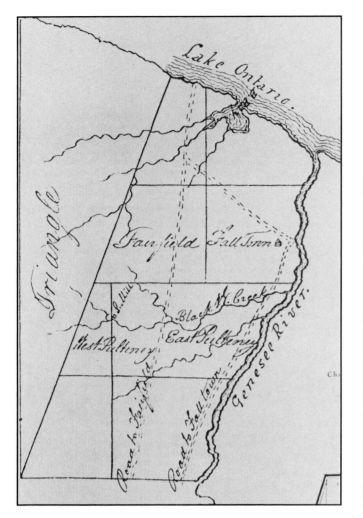

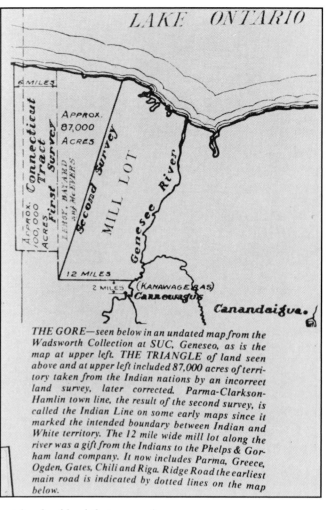

THE GORE—seen below in an undated map from the Wadsworth Collection at SUC, Geneseo, as is the map at upper left. THE TRIANGLE of land seen above and at upper left included 87,000 acres of territory taken from the Indian nations by an incorrect land survey, later corrected. Parma-Clarkson-Hamlin town line, the result of the second survey, is called the Indian Line on some early maps since it marked the intended boundary between Indian and White territory. The 12 mile wide mill lot along the river was a gift from the Indians to the Phelps & Gorham land company. It now includes Parma, Greece, Ogden, Gates, Chili and Riga. Ridge Road the earliest main road is indicated by dotted lines on the map below.

Map of the triangle of land that was accidentally included in the original survey of the Phelps and Gorham purchase. After the Senecas protested, the land was resurveyed so that the western boundary paralleled the Genesee River as the Seneca Indians had intended.
From the Office of the County Historian

A map of the Phelps and Gorham purchase showing the location of the mill seat.
From the Office of the County Historian

Oliver Phelps (1749-1809) from an oil painting in the Ontario County Court House in Canandaigua.
From the Office of the City Historian

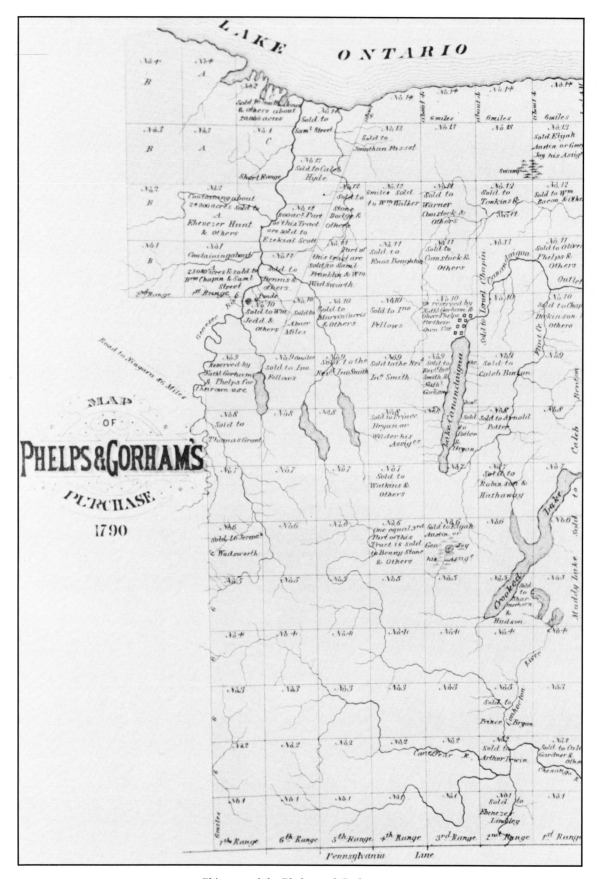

This map of the Phelps and Gorham purchase in 1790 shows the 2.6 million acres purchased by them after it was divided into lots.
From the Rochester Public Library

A portrait of Charles Williamson. Inflation left Oliver Phelps and Nathaniel Gorham unable to meet payments on their huge purchase so they sold much of the land to Robert Morris who in turn sold it to William Pulteney Associates. Pulteney hired Col. Charles Williamson as land agent in 1791. Williamson's Series of Letters From a Gentleman to His Friend *gave the earliest detailed description of the beauty and potential of the Genesee country. It was published in Albany in 1798. In 1800 Williamson personally guided Nathaniel Rochester, William Fitzhugh, and Charles Carroll to the falls of the Genesee River where they saw the ruins of Ebenezer (Indian) Allan's abandoned mills.*
From a portrait in the Davenport Library in Bath, New York; from the Office of the City Historian

Mary Jemison was known to early settlers as the "White Woman of the Genesee." Her life was recorded by James Seaver in A Narrative of the Life of Mrs. Mary Jemison, *published in 1833. She was born in 1743 to Irish parents aboard a ship bound for America. She lived on the family farm in Pennsylvania until she was fifteen when a Shawnee raiding party killed most of her family and the Senecas adopted her. She lived as a Seneca, married twice, and raised her children in their villages. She recalled Gen. John Sullivan's march in 1779, the hardships suffered among the Indians, and other stories of Indian life and their relationships with white settlers. She lived on her farm on the Gardeau Flats in what is now Letchworth Park and died at the Buffalo Creek Reservation at her daughter's home.*
From the Rochester Public Library

Chapter Two

Enos Stone was the first permanent settler on the east side of the Genesee River. When he built this frame cabin in 1812 to replace his log cabin, it became the first frame building on the east side of the river. He probably cut the boards from his own sawmill near the present South and Broad streets. This photograph was taken in 1899 by Charles Howard. The building is no longer standing.
From the Rochester Historical Society and the Rochester Public Library

CARVING A VILLAGE FROM THE WILDERNESS

THE MILLS AT THE FALLS

In the summer of 1789, Ebenezer (Indian) Allan began to build a sawmill on the One Hundred Acre Tract. It was nearly winter before he was able to cut the boards to build the gristmill. The thirty foot by twenty-six foot gristmill stood between the present Aqueduct and Graves streets on the south side of Main Street.

John Maude, a British traveler, said Allan, with the help of several Indians, dressed the two six-hundred-pound millstones from local red and grey granite boulders. The stones were 3', 9" in diameter, from 9" to 11" thick, with a center hole 9" in diameter. Only one side of the crude stones was leveled.

Allan's knowledge of milling was evidently limited, for Maude noted that "the gristmill . . . (was) very ill constructed, . . . (was) erected too near the bed of the river, and the race (was) . . . so improperly managed that it (was) . . . dry in summer and liable to back water in the winter." The mill ground only ten bushels a day, but Maude thought if it was well managed, it could have ground sixty. Settlers from as far away as Canandaigua hauled their grain over the rugged roads to the mill, but there were so few settlers, that the mills were neglected and settlers began to travel to Rundecut where there was a mill at the projected city of Tryon. In 1791, Allan left the mills in the charge of his brother-in-law Christopher Dugan, and they were soon abandoned.

Allan married several women, and through one of them with Indian land rights, had become the owner of a farm near Scottsville. When he abandoned the mills, he returned to his farm. He not only had many Indian friends and relatives, he was a gunsmith and blacksmith to them. Allan met with mixed reviews, however, for historian John DeVoy characterized him as "a bandit captain or a pirate chief." He said Allan was a murderer, a forger, a thief, and "was withal a tory in the Revolution."

Allan visited Mary Jemison, the "white woman of the Genesee," on numerous occasions and she did not like the influence that he had over her son. She did not feel he should be trusted.

In 1792 Benjamin Barton bought the mill site. He sold it two years later to Sir William Pulteney's London Associates who hired Charles Williamson as land agent. Williamson thought that by moving the mill to higher ground, it would be out of the way of ice and backwater and by moving the race, the water would not only maintain a summer level of six feet, it would allow logs to be floated to the sawmill and river rafts to load and unload at the mill.

Williamson never made the improvements, though he hired Col. Josiah Fish to operate Allan's old mills. Fish moved his family into a three-sided lean-to built against the side of a rock ledge and there the first three white children were born within the area of the present Rochester. Finding mill business still infrequent, Fish, too, had abandoned the mills by 1803.

THE ONE HUNDRED ACRE TRACT

In 1803, three Maryland investors, Nathaniel Rochester, William Fitzhugh, and Charles Carroll purchased the abandoned mill site recognizing the potential of the fourteen-foot falls. The site on the Genesee River offered unusual commercial opportunities. Goods could be sent three miles north around the three falls where they could be loaded on ships for a six-mile voyage to the Port of Genesee and on to Canadian ports on Lake Ontario and European markets beyond. Riverboats could push against the current for sixty miles south of the mill seat where forwarders connected to the Susquehanna Valley in Pennsylvania, or after a difficult thirty-mile portage, connected with the Ohio River.

But with few settlers in the Genesee Valley, it was still too early to develop the One Hundred Acre Tract. Settlers stopped at Canandaigua and Avon or Geneva along the southern turnpike rather than venture into unbroken wilderness. Rochester, Fitzhugh, and Carroll did not attempt to develop the land until 1809 when Colonel Rochester decided to move his family to his land in Dansville in search of better opportunities for his sons. Though the Embargo and Nonintercourse Acts depressed trade in Maryland because it forbade trade with warring France and England, the act increased illegal trade with Canada and this made the Genesee River an important carrier of exports from the south.

Settlers scattered about the Genesee country began to ship their grain and potash from the Indian Landing at Irondequoit Bay or Charlotte at the mouth of the river. When Colonel Rochester saw in 1810 that there was so much activity on the river, he began the next year to survey the land he owned on the west side of the river and to divide it into lots. Enos Stone, the first permanent settler on the east side of the river, was hired as land agent, giving him an interest in, rather than competition with, the new development.

The site offered the further advantage of being on an important Indian trail and fording place over which the state built what became the Main Street Bridge in 1811. Bridge work was in progress at the fording place on the site of the present Main Street Bridge when Colonel Rochester learned that Francis and Matthew Brown had the bridge site moved to their two hundred-acre tract just north of the One Hundred Acre Tract. Rochester persuaded the legislature to make the route that crossed the river a state road and to redirect it through his tract. The bridge was important, for the only other bridge on the Genesee River was twenty miles south at Avon (then Hartford). Hundreds of settlers in need of supplies would be expected to arrive from the east to trade at the settlement on the One Hundred Acre Tract on the west side of the river.

THE WAR OF 1812

Unfortunately, the settlement was delayed by the threat of British attack during the War of 1812. Several times the British threatened to destroy port improvements at the mouth of the river. News of the burning of Lewiston frightened settlers and the few men who were resident took up arms for the local protection committee. The river crossing at the One Hundred Acre Tract was active as a meeting and supply center for the militia. Despite the delayed settlement, when the war ended there were over three hundred settlers on the tract and a gristmill, two sawmills, and a tavern.

When the war ended, shoemakers, tinsmiths, farmers, tailors, and printers purchased lots. Businesses constructed along Buffalo Street (now West Main) supplied customers who worked their way among the tree stumps on the newly cleared road. The new buildings stood in clearings still surrounded by forest.

Hamlet Scrantom was the first permanent settler. He traveled with his family from Lewis County pulling their covered wagon with a double yoke of oxen and a horse. The roads through Geneva, Canandaigua, and Pittsford were rough, but traveling near their new settlement was even more difficult. The family arrived two miles south of their lot at the river rapids (near the present University of Rochester). They were ferried across the river by Isaac Castle, where they were invited to spend the night in the tavern at Castletown.

The next morning Scrantom and his three sons traveled the path along the west bank of the river to the unfinished bridge (Main Street). A half-completed cabin awaited them, so they crossed the river on the framework of the bridge and Enos Stone, Rochester's land agent, allowed them to live in his abandoned cabin on the east side. It was July before Scrantom could finish his cabin.

Scrantom's experience was not unusual. Friends said sad goodbyes to those setting out for the Genesee country for they expected never to see them again. All they knew of this country, one pioneer said, was wolves and Indians. But the land was settled quickly after the war of 1812 and settlers were not long alone.

There were other settlements along the river: Matthew and Francis Brown's Frankfort tract just north of the One Hundred Acre Tract, King's Landing at the Lower Falls, and Charlotte at the mouth of the river. Charlotte and King's Landing on the west side both had shipping facilities.

The One Hundred Acre Tract was becoming a mill town. It was dependent on Charlotte and King's Landing for lake access. A portage road was soon built along the west side of the river.

Charlotte was built on the mouth of the river at the point made the official port of entry in 1805. A lighthouse, built in 1822, replaced the two old butternut trees that sailors called the "pilot trees," for they marked the entrance to the river's mouth when lined up. Charlotte later boasted improved piers that controlled the migrating sand bars and waves. In 1805, Canandaigua merchants built a road from Canandaigua through the new city of Tryon on Irondequoit Bay from which they portaged their goods to Charlotte. Migrating sand at the mouth of the Bay, the loss of trade with warring Canada, the death of owner John Tryon, and the arrival of the news of the Erie Canal at Rochesterville as well as the designation of Charlotte as the official port of entry combined to eventually end shipping at Tryon, but Charlotte remained a busy port.

King's Landing on the west side of the river at the steamboat landing and Carthage on the east side, were the southernmost lake ports on the Genesee River. King's Landing and Carthage on the other side of the river were built along the Indian trail that became a state road (Ridge Road, sometimes called Lewiston Road) between the county seat at Canandaigua and the Niagara River.

In 1818, at the fording place near the base of the falls, Canandaigua promoters of Carthage built a single arch wooden bridge 190 feet above the river from cliffs on each side. The wooden structure was an engineering marvel that rivaled any bridge in Europe, visitors said. It was 714' long with a 352' arch. The bridge was guaranteed to stand one year, but in the fifteenth month, the arch of the bridge snapped under its own weight. With the bridge destroyed, Charlotte gained an edge in lake shipping. Schooners traveling up the river to Carthage or King's Landing did not always have enough wind to drive them against the current. Men and animals pulled on ropes from the shore to bring the ships in. Certainly ships going only as far as Charlotte at the mouth of the river, had an advantage over Carthage, but Rochesterville, with its milling and lake access, soon outgrew all the other settlements.

ROCHESTER BECOMES THE NEW VILLAGE

In 1817, when the Brown brothers' Frankfort Tract was annexed by the One Hundred Acre Tract, the new village of Rochesterville increased to 655 acres with seven hundred residents.

Rochesterville had the potential to become the economic hub of the Genesee Valley since, in 1809, the state legislature decided to build a canal from Lake Erie to the Hudson River's outlet to the Atlantic to capture the increasing number of shipments then being sent to Canada. Rochesterville was fortunate, for its topography made it a better route for the canal than through the older, thriving settlements along the turnpike (today's Route 20) at Geneva, Canandaigua, Avon, or at nearby Bath. Colonel Rochester had moved his family in 1817 from Dansville to Rochesterville to give a firm hand to the direction of the rapidly growing village. In the six years since it was laid out in lots, Rochesterville had grown into a mill town with a competitive edge over all of the other Genesee River settlements.

The village was growing so rapidly that in 1821, Colonel Rochester was able to persuade the legislature to create Monroe County. Previous attempts to form a new county were resisted by politicians representing both Canandaigua and Batavia, the county seats of Ontario and Genesee Counties, but the increasing population of the Genesee country and the joint movement by Rochesterville, Geneseo, and Lyons to subdivide could not be resisted, and the new counties of Monroe, Livingston, and Wayne were formed.

The Monroe County Court House was built in 1822 on a swampy lot laid out near the Four Corners. The site was chosen over Elisha Johnson's Square (Washington Square) and Francis and Matthew Brown's Square (Brown's Square), all originally laid as potential sites for a courthouse. Nathaniel Rochester became the first county clerk.

With the new Bank of Rochester chartered in 1824, builders and shippers would no longer have to approach the Canandaigua bank for loans. Investors as far away as New York found Rochesterville a good investment. Certainly the availability of money stimulated growth.

In 1818, one year before Rochesterville became a village, the Rochester *Gazette*, the first weekly newspaper, began publishing. Two years later, Everard Peck published the *Telegraph*. In the rapidly growing community, there were many opinions and many newspapers to express them. Henry O'Reilly began to publish the *Rochester*

Daily Advertiser in 1826 and shortly before, the *Rochester Observer* and the *Liberal Advocate* began. They were soon joined by agricultural newspapers as well.

Newspapers in these early days made little distinction, if any, between editorial comment and news stories. Articles on political events, antislavery speeches, and the anti-Mason stories that circulated after the kidnapping and death of William Morgan, had to be read in conjunction with other less biased reports to obtain a balanced story.

The kidnapping and murder in 1827 of William Morgan, a former Mason who decided to publish the secrets of the society, set off an anti-Masonic movement that lasted for years. *Rochester Telegraph* editor Thurlow Weed used his newspaper to exploit the hostilities of the people against the influential secret society, and by 1829, his campaign elected him to the state assembly in Albany.

The *Rochester Observer* supported the temperance movement and the revivals of the Rev. Charles Finney who preached several sermons every day for several months in 1830, so affecting the Rochester area, that hundreds of people flocked to churches to be saved, idle amusements declined, and taverns were less frequented. Finney visited Rochester several times between 1830 and 1855. Later newspaper editors used their newspapers to support or condemn social and political causes and to drive home the message of the religious revivals of the 1830s.

But the influence of the revivals eventually diminished, though the temperance and antislavery movements seemed to have gained an energy and dedication that lasted until the attainment of their goals.

THE ERIE CANAL

In 1797, less than a decade after the Phelps and Gorham purchase, New York's Governor DeWitt Clinton asked the legislature to finance the construction of a canal to encourage the settlement and development of northern and western New York. The newly formed Niagara Canal Company found a canal between Lake Ontario and Lake Erie too costly, but after several local canals proved successful, the construction of the Erie Canal was funded by the state legislature. Five million dollars was earmarked for the 363-mile-long canal. After much study, it was designed to be forty feet wide and four feet deep, controlled by seventy-seven locks, ninety feet in width.

By 1817 when Canal construction began, Rochesterville was rapidly developing. The War of 1812 had delayed settlement, but the villagers were now draining swamps, building homes, cutting out races, and operating mills.

Most people, even its planners, were surprised by the success of the canal. Jesse Hawley said after the canal operated for a decade, that "No single act—no public measure—except the Declaration of Independence and the formation of the U.S. Constitution has done so much to promote public prosperity and produce a new era in the history of the country as the construction of the Erie Canal."

Just as DeWitt Clinton had hoped, the canal helped to settle the densely forested, swampy western and northern sections of the state. Trade developed on open sections of the canal even before it was fully completed. So many settlers came, in fact, that the population of Rochesterville jumped from 2,700 in 1822 to 7,670 in 1826 when the canal had been open officially for only one year.

The flurry of activity presented an air of confusion to many European visitors. The docks were busy with passengers and tons of grain, flour, bricks, stone, and other materials were loaded and unloaded from the canal boats and freight wagons. On May 31, 1825, the *Rochester Telegraph* reported, "Our basins and wharves presented yesterday morning the appearances of a bustling commercial town—forwards and clerks, wagons and boatmen, all confusion and hurry; boats arriving and departing constantly."

The Erie Canal officially opened in 1825, but as parts of the east side opened from 1823, anxious shippers loaded goods on it. In the first ten days of the season in 1823, Rochester already had shipped out 10,450 barrels of flour, and 417 barrels of pork and potash on fifty-eight boats. Forty-five boats brought into Rochester 4,000 gallons of beer, 2,300 gallons of whiskey and even New England oysters.

The canal officially opened on October 26, 1825. It now stretched 363 miles from the Hudson river at Albany to Lake Erie at Buffalo. When the boats left Buffalo to begin the first official trip the full length of the canal, cannons spaced along the canal began to fire, signaling that the boats were moving eastward. When the people heard the cannons, they fired theirs off, too. All along the canal and down the Hudson River from west to east cannons were fired until only an hour and twenty minutes later the message of the signal cannon in Buffalo reached New York City. The boats, pulled by mules that were changed every few hours, moved very slowly at about three miles an hour. It took the *Seneca Chief* carrying the governor's party, nearly two days to reach Rochester.

People stood along the banks of the canal to watch the opening ceremonies. They did not mind that it was raining. They cheered as they watched the governor's flotilla moving slowly toward their village while the Rochester Band began to play.

The *Seneca Chief* drew slowly into a westside basin where a salute fired by a militia company signaled the village band to play. A Rochester boat called the *Young Lion of the West* met the *Seneca Chief* on the west side at Jonathan Child's Basin.

"Who goes there?" called a man from the *Young Lion of the West.*

Our brothers from the west on the waters of the great lakes," answered someone from the governor's boat.

The crowd quieted and strained to hear the voices. "By what means have they come so far?" asked a man of the *Young Lion of the West.*

"By the grand Erie Canal," answered the voice on the *Seneca Chief.*

"By what authority, and by whom was such a great piece of work done?" asked the man on the *Young Lion of the West.*

"By the authority and energy of the patriotic people of the state of New York," answered the man on the *Seneca Chief.*

Hundreds of people joining in the celebration must have swelled with pride, for many had helped to build the canal and aqueduct with their own hands. The governor and scores of officials prayed at the First Presbyterian Church near the canal and officials made speeches about the importance of the canal. Later Governor Clinton joined officials for dinner at the Mansion House. That night there were fireworks, and many jubilant toasts and parties celebrating the opening of the canal, but no one that night could have predicted the dramatic economic boom that Rochester was soon to experience.

The profile of Ebenezer (Indian) Allan, the "Old Man of the Genesee," was carved by the elements into the rock ledge at the Lower Falls near the Driving Park Avenue Bridge. The profile changes as pieces of rock fall away and the rain and wind erode it.
From a postcard at the Rochester Public Library

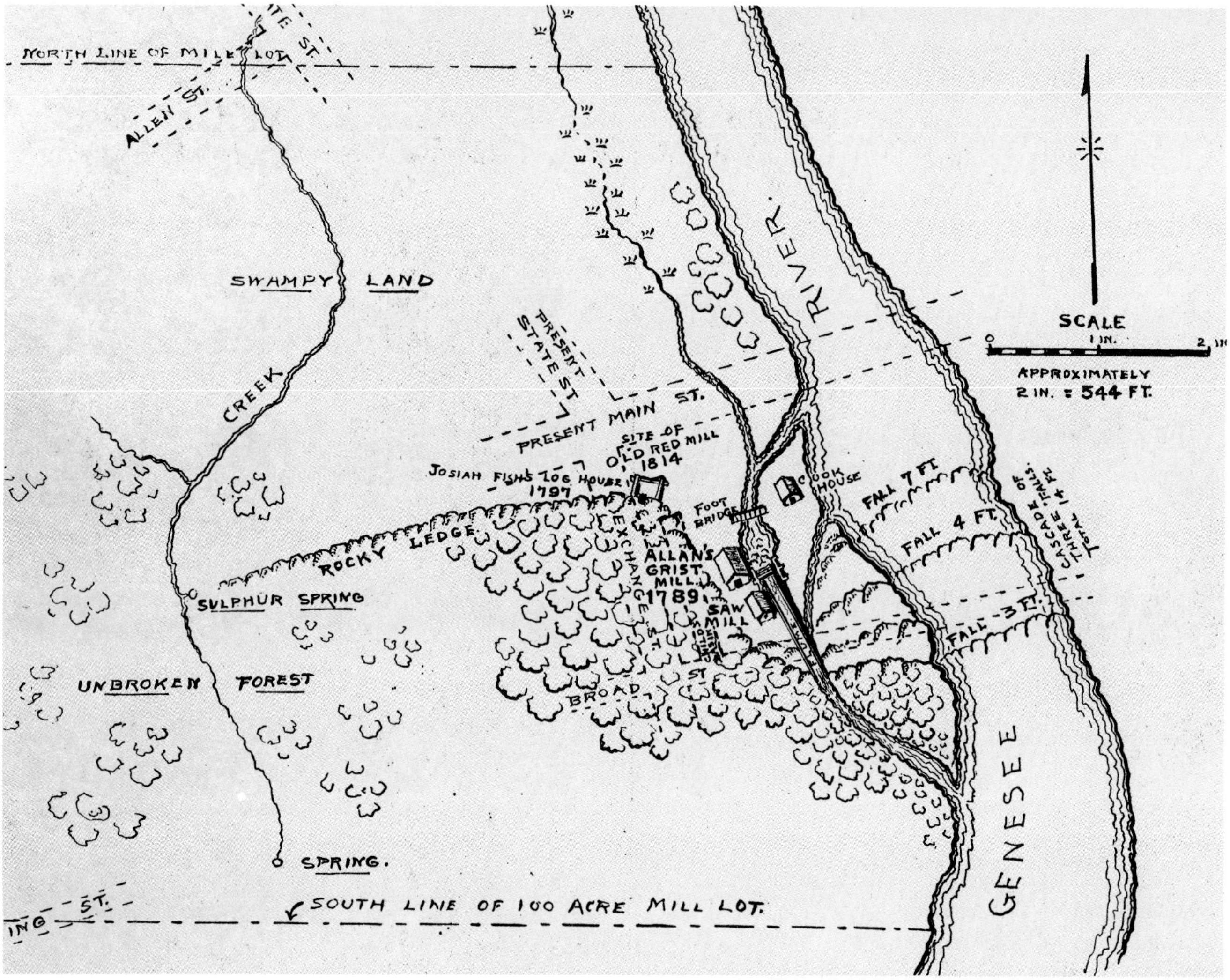
NORTH LINE OF MILL LOT
ALLEN ST.
SWAMPY LAND
CREEK
PRESENT STATE ST
PRESENT MAIN ST.
SITE OF OLD RED MILL 1814
JOSIAH FISH'S LOG HOUSE 1797
ROCKY LEDGE
EXCHANGE
FOOT BRIDGE
COOK HOUSE
ALLAN'S GRIST MILL 1789
SAW MILL
RIVER
SCALE
1 IN.
APPROXIMATELY
2 IN. = 544 FT.
FALL 7 FT.
FALL 4 FT.
FALL 3 FT.
SULPHUR SPRING
UNBROKEN FOREST
BROAD ST
GENESEE
SPRING.
SOUTH LINE OF 100 ACRE MILL LOT.
ING ST.

Ebenezer (Indian) Allan built a sawmill and a gristmill on the One Hundred Acre Tract in 1789. The falls were not as high as the other three falls along the Genesee, but the mills were located near the Indian fording place at today's Broad Street Bridge, which allowed greater access to the mills. Though there were Indians scattered around Corn Hill, near the springs, at the fording places, at the mills, and at the Lower Falls, the main Indian villages were located around the Finger Lakes so there were not enough Indians or settlers to keep the mills running and they were soon abandoned. The settlers did not venture into the wilderness. Though Josiah Fish tried a few years later to operate the mills, he too found that there were not enough customers. Fish built his three-sided cabin against a rock ledge that later settlers said held a large rattlesnake den. The mills did not operate until Nathaniel Rochester's son, Thomas, built a mill over the old Allan race around 1813.
Map drawn by Maj. Wheeler C. Case with Morley Turpin; from the Rochester Public Library

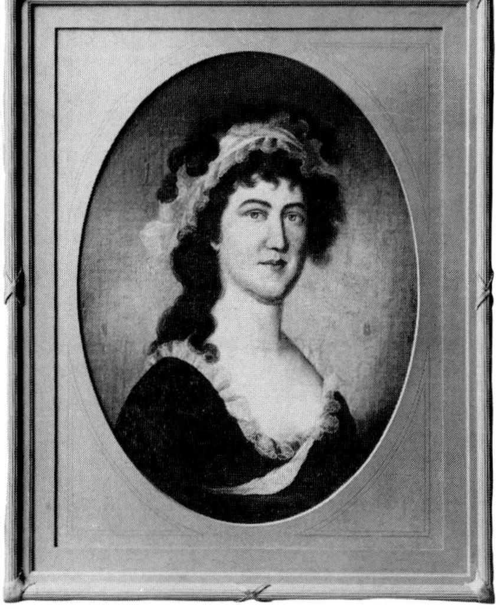

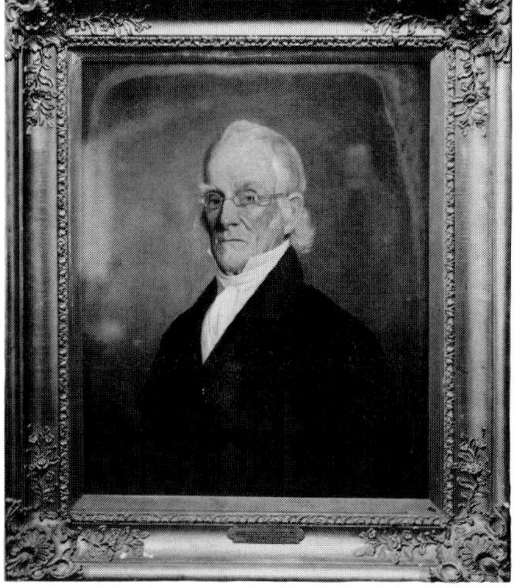

Col. Nathaniel Rochester (1752-1831) and his wife Sophia, bought the One Hundred Acre site of Ebenezer (Indian) Allan's abandoned mills in 1803 with partners William Fitzhugh and Charles Carroll. On an inspection tour to the falls in 1810, Col. Rochester saw heavily loaded wagons and flatboats waiting along the river to ship from the port at Charlotte. Rochester had the land surveyed and laid out in lots the following year. He hired Enos Stone to sell lots, but the War of 1812 not only slowed settlement, many of the residents left the river and mouth in fear of the British who threatened to destroy lake improvements and landings. Settlement after the war was rapid. Competition between settlements along the river continued until the opening of the Erie Canal made Rochester the economic crossroads of the Genesee River Valley. The Colonel moved his family to Bloomfield twenty miles south of the present Rochester where he could travel more frequently to the new settlement. He came to live in Rochesterville in 1817, the year he helped to found St. Luke's Episcopal Church.

Rochester persuaded Matthew and Francis Brown to plot their Frankfort village streets to line up with those of the One Hundred Acre Tract to form Rochesterville in 1817.
From the Rochester Historical Society and the Rochester Public Library

When the Main Street Bridge was proposed over the Genesee River, many in the state legislature complained that the Genesee country was a god-forsaken wilderness. Many thought the bridge crossing at Avon twenty miles south of the present Rochester was adequate, but many settlers were beginning to cross at the fording places and some settlers were nearly swept over the falls by swift currents. One farmer and his team were killed when they were carried over the falls in 1805. When DeWitt Clinton toured the falls before the construction of the Erie Canal began, he noted in his diary that the bridge then under construction was substantial.
From W. H. McIntosh's History of Monroe County, Rochester, 1877; from the Rochester Public Library

The home of Nathaniel Wheeler built in 1818 on Hooker's Flats on the east side of the Genesee River near Carthage was typical of early homes.
From the Rochester Historical Society and the Rochester Public Library

Hamlet Scrantom arrived in 1812, but found his west side cabin not yet completed. He lived in the cabin abandoned by Enos Stone on the east side of the river until he could move. Hamlet Scrantom was the first permanent settler in the One Hundred Acre Tract after Col. Rochester laid it out in lots.
Drawing from the Rochester Historical Society and the Rochester Public Library

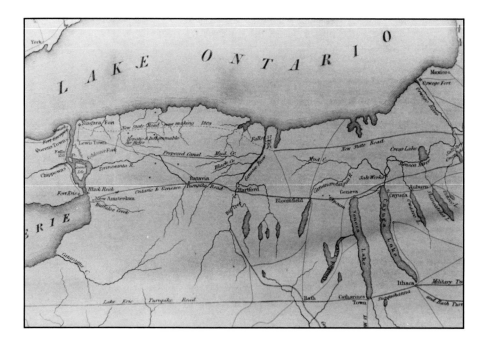

Most of the early settlers were settling along the turnpike (now Route 20) at Geneva, Hartford, Bloomfield, or farther south at Bath. The northern Genesee River region was a wilderness few wanted to venture into, especially after the War of 1812 began and the British ships on Lake Ontario threatened the ports and landings below the falls and at the mouth of the Genesee River. But roads were being built. This 1809 map shows the new state road built almost to the river and under construction on the west side. The bridge at Carthage, built in 1819, connected these two roads for fifteen months.
Map from Thomas Cooper's A Ride to Niagara in 1809; from the Office of the City Historian

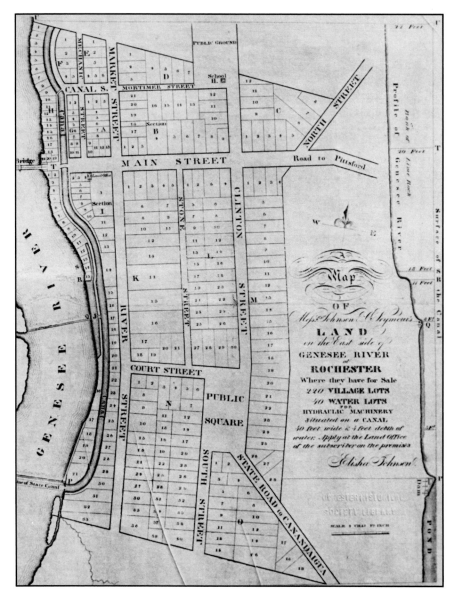

Elisha Johnson and James Seymour divided this land into 220 village lots and 40 mill sites in 1817. The competition to become the site for the courthouse of the proposed county motivated Johnson as well as Frankfort developers to set aside a courthouse square and a public square, but in 1821 when Monroe County was formed it was Nathaniel Rochester's more centrally located Court House Square that was selected as the site for the new courthouse. Frankfort's Brown Square and Johnson's Washington Square are used today as city parks.
From the Rochester Public Library

The Port at Carthage around 1838 as it appeared in Henry O'Reilly's Sketches of Rochester.

This engraving of the Port of Rochester at Charlotte appeared in Frank Leslie's Illustrated Weekly *in April of 1856. It was drawn from an ambrotype by Whitney of Rochester. At this time, Charlotte at the mouth of the river was important because of its access to the lake and its rail connections with the city of Rochester seven miles south. Steamers with international trade arrived and departed daily from this port. Charlotte was a growing, thriving settlement before the Erie Canal made Rochester the center of much of the shipping and commerce.*
Courtesy of William T. Davis

Elisha Johnson began to blast his race in 1817 on the Fourth of July, helping to celebrate the holiday with the noise of industry and construction that made Rochester a boom town. Johnson was a creative developer. Lacking adequate transport to the lake for his mill products, he built a three-mile track and ran the first local horse-drawn railroad north to the landing at Carthage in 1832.
From the Rochester Historical Society and the Rochester Public Library

Dr. Jonah Brown arrived in Rochesterville in 1813 from Columbia County, New York. He set up a practice and began calling on patients on horseback. One day, he recalled years later, he was visiting a patient near the rapids (near the University of Rochester) when "he barely escaped falling into the claws of a panther . . . ." With the frequent outbreaks of Genesee Fever and epidemics of smallpox and cholera, he often acted as nurse, cook, and doctor. Sometimes whole families were ill at the same time. Medicine was difficult to keep in supply until the Erie Canal later made shipments from the east more regular, so early doctors concocted their own prescriptions.
From the Rochester Historical Society and the Rochester Public Library

The Carthage Railroad and Steam Boat
House was built in 1818 to accommodate
weary travelers over the Ridge Road. The
new state road was partially finished
around 1809. Ridge Road was so busy
with travelers and settlers that hardly an
hour went by when a wagon or a horse-
man was not passing by the house. It was
conveniently located at the east end of
the famous wooden bridge near the Lower
Falls at Carthage. The rear section of the
building was removed in 1888, destroying
the first few letters of the name painted
on the side of the building which was demolished in 1931. Many such structures
that dated from the pioneer period survived into the twentieth century.
From the Rochester Historical Society and
the Rochester Public Library

Abram Hanford was one of seven brothers
who bought the old King's Landing, renamed it Hanford's Landing and conducted a thriving shipping business from
the Genesee River to the lake. Abram
built a tavern on Hanford's Landing Road
off Lake Avenue in 1809. Because there
was no sawmill nearby at this early date,
there is some speculation that an earlier
building stood on this site before the tavern pictured. Gov. DeWitt Clinton stayed
there in 1810 when he traveled with the
Canal Commissioners exploring the route
of the proposed Erie Canal. He remarked
that Hanford carried on a considerable
trade with Canada. Two years later this
tavern was a rendevous point for American soldiers and sailors during the War of
1812. This building was photographed by
James Angle in 1883, the year before it
was torn down. The tavern was also
called the Old Lion Inn.
From the Rochester Public Library

Brown's Race was the most active of all
the races in the present Rochester.
Matthew and Francis Brown built the
race at the Main (Upper) Falls with
Thomas Mumford in 1816. The race was
cut through rock and the tail race emptied into the river from the mills ninety
six feet above. The race is still used to
generate electricity by the Rochester Gas
and Electric Company. These mills in
1880 were, from left to right; Ferguson
and Lewis (Old Whitney Mills), Moseley
and Motley (Mill B), Smith and Sherman
(Old Frankfort Mills), Irving Mills (Stone
and Campbell), Moseley and Motley (Mill
A), People's Custom Mill (Mertz and Co.),
Shawmut Mill (Whitney and Wilson), and
Washington Mill (J.A. Hinds and Co.).
From the Rochester Public Library

Elkanah Watson was one of the biggest supporters of the Erie Canal. It is largely owing to his advocacy that the Erie Canal was successfully built. The Erie Canal made Rochester a boom town and overcame Rochester's lack of easy access to lake shipping.
From the Rochester Public Library

Thurlow Weed (1797-1882), the editor of the Rochester Telegraph, was elected to the state assembly on an antimasonry platform. He was a leader in the Whig and Republican parties. Because he arrived in Rochester in 1822 and witnessed its rapid growth, his biography, The Life and Times of Thurlow Weed, gives a good view of the growth and development of early Rochester.
From the Rochester Public Library

St. Luke's Episcopal Church was established by Nathaniel Rochester and other congregants in 1817. Worship was begun in a wooden church built earlier behind this stone church built in 1824. This photograph, taken in 1917, shows the building substantially unchanged in nearly one hundred years. It still stands today, its architecture contrasting with the modern, larger buildings that have since grown up around it. In January 1988 it merged with St. Simon's Cyrene Church. It is on the National Register of Historic Places.
From the Rochester Public Library

ROCHESTER EVENING ADVERTISER.

VOLUME I. ROCHESTER, WEDNESDAY EVENING, JANUARY 2, 1833. NUMBER 2.

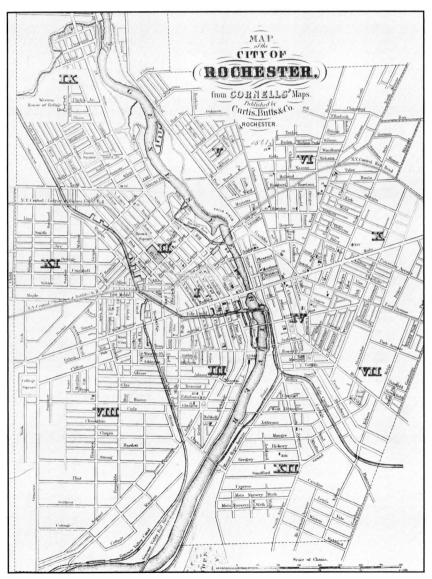

A view of Rochester and the Erie Canal from the west drawn by Charles Magnus in 1853. The aqueduct over the Genesee River is barely visible in the upper center of the drawing. Buffalo Street in the center is built up over the entire route, even on the south side over the river. Court House Square is visible in the center between the Canal and Main Street. In the lower left corner, the Rochester Novelty Works is visible with the cupola.
From the Rochester Public Library

The route of the Erie Canal is shown in this 1861 map of the city by Silas Cornell. A second Erie Canal aqueduct was built to replace the first leaking sandstone aqueduct in 1842, moving the duct slightly to reduce the sharp curve of the east end. The Genesee Valley Canal is shown connecting to the Erie Canal.
From the Rochester Public Library

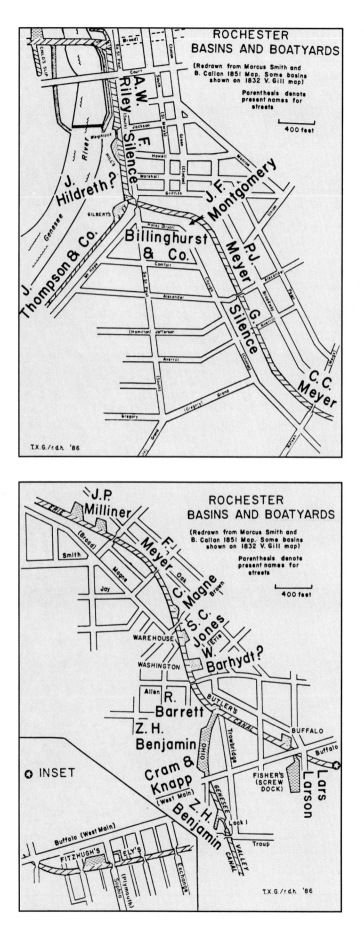

Maps of the Rochester basins and boatyards. The loading docks and boat building enterprises were essential to canal operations.
From the 1832 map by V. Gill and the 1851 map of Marcus Smith and B. Callan; redrawn by Thomas X. Grasso in 1986.

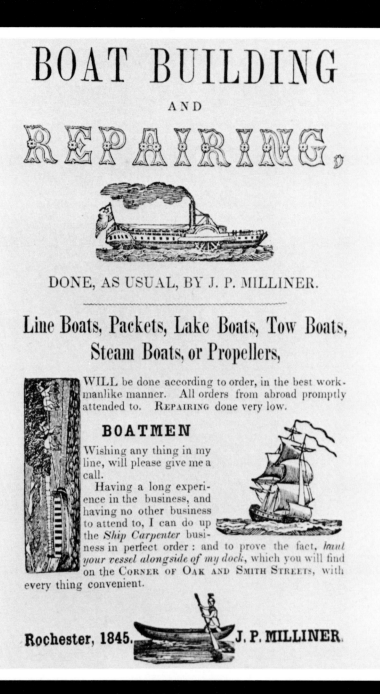

BOAT BUILDING

AND

REPAIRING,

DONE, AS USUAL, BY J. P. MILLINER.

Line Boats, Packets, Lake Boats, Tow Boats, Steam Boats, or Propellers,

WILL be done according to order, in the best work-manlike manner. All orders from abroad promptly attended to. REPAIRING done very low.

BOATMEN

Wishing any thing in my line, will please give me a call.

Having a long experience in the business, and having no other business to attend to, I can do up the *Ship Carpenter* business in perfect order : and to prove the fact, *haul your vessel alongside of my dock*, which you will find on the CORNER OF OAK AND SMITH STREETS, with every thing convenient.

Rochester, 1845.   J. P. MILLINER.

From the 1845 Rochester City Directory.

Chapter Three

The Charlotte Lighthouse was built in 1822. The keeper's house was built in 1863 of brick. The light shining through the fog or dark of night was a welcome sight to many ship captains seeking entry into the mouth of the Genesee River. Before the lighthouse was built, sailors looked for two butternut trees near the mouth. When the trees were lined up, they guided sailors safely into the natural harbor. Sailors called the trees the "pilot trees." They were destroyed when piers and other improvements were put in.

Photograph by George Archibald in the collection of the Rochester Public Library

FROM VILLAGE TO CITY

A TRAVELER'S NOTES ON A BOOM TOWN

Rochester was not yet two decades old when the budding author Nathaniel Hawthorne visited in the fall of 1830. Traveling by the new Erie Canal, he, like other visitors, expected to see a boom town—a town hurriedly built of wood. But instead he described permanent brick and stone buildings with pavements worn by hundreds of passing carriages and boots. He wrote:

> Its edifices are of dusky brick and of stone that will not be grayer in a hundred years than now . . . . It is impossible to look at its worn pavements and conceive how lately the forest leaves have been swept away.

> The whole streets, sidewalks and centre were crowded with pedestrians, horsemen, stagecoaches, gigs, light wagons and heavy ox-teams, all hurrying, trotting, rattling, and rumbling, in a throng that passed continually, but never passed away. Here, a country wife was selecting a churn from several gaily painted ones on a sunny sidewalk; there a farmer was bartering his produce; and in two or three places, a crowd of people were showering bids on a vociferous auctioneer. I saw a great wagon and ox-chain knocked off (sold) to a very pretty woman . . . .

> The number of public houses benefitted the flow of temporary population; some were farmers' taverns—cheap, homely and comfortable; others were magnificent hotels with negro waiters, gentlemanly landlords in black broadcloth and foppish barkeepers in Broad-

way coats with chased gold watches in their waistcoat pockets.

The rapid growth of the village brought increased demands for water, sewerage, and other services. In 1834 Rochester incorporated as a city. Jonathan Child, Nathaniel Rochester's son-in-law, was chosen as the first mayor.

Life in the city was becoming more pleasant. Many roads between villages were completed. In 1837, the first steam locomotive in the city ran between Rochester and Tonawanda for the Tonawanda Railroad Company. It chugged its way to Churchville, Brockport, Batavia, and back in a single day. Other lines began. By 1834 three stage lines were also running and steamboats and sailing vessels left the Port of Genesee daily with stage lines making connections with the city. The Erie Canal carried hundreds of travelers every week.

Farmers too could travel into the city over improved roads. Shipments of farm produce were easier to get to market and to canal and lake docks. And almost anything needed by a farmer could be obtained in the city. Tools and equipment were not only brought in by canal and ship, they were manufactured at factories along the river. Farmers ate and slept in Rochester hotels and found amusement now and then. Much of what was once made on the farm could now be bought in the city. Women were able to buy imported yard goods and ready-made clothing and shoes.

Coal was brought by canal to the city by Jonathan Child for use in the factories and homes.

By 1848, the Municipal Gas Works began to serve a small number of homes and street lamps.

In 1847, the first Pioneer Festival was held at the Blossom Hotel. More than fifty pioneers and their sons attended this banquet to reminisce about the city's growth and their part in it. They recalled the changes in government, travel, schools, churches, and the kinds of people settling in the city. They expressed confidence in the city's future growth and importance.

THE MILLERS AT THE GRINDSTONES

Rochester was in the midst of the wheat belt by the 1830s. Millers worked late into the season grinding wheat and other grains and shipping thousands of barrels by lake and canal every year. Milling was the dominant industry.

Other factories tanned leather, produced edge tools, sheet metal, barrels, pianos, tobacco, wagons, and even fire engines. There were half a dozen canal boatyards by 1838. Thousands of newcomers easily found jobs in these factories.

EARLY AMUSEMENTS

If it was not an educational or moral performance, Rochester's largely New England migrants shunned the amusements of the early village. The single theatre struggled to stay open for a while, but in 1838, after Rev. Charles Finney's religious exhortations, historian Henry O'Reilly proudly wrote, "Theatres and circuses cannot now be found in Rochester . . . . The theatre was converted into a livery stable, and the circus into a chandler's shop." He and others like him, were concerned that idle amusement distracted young minds from improving through the increasing number of literary and scientific societies and the privately owned Rochester Museum.

But the circuses that had skirted the village earlier began to attract large crowds to Falls Field and other large vacant fields around Rochester. The circuses were watched carefully by the press that reported their moral and educational exhibits of Biblical sketches and exotic animals.

In 1829, famous falls jumper Sam Patch jumped from Brown's Island into the water below the Upper Falls. Jumping with his animal companion, a huge bear, Sam Patch had made quite a name for himself in a few short years. In 1829 he attracted such a crowd on his first jump that he advertised another jump on Friday, November 13 from a high platform that raised his earlier jump over the falls to 125 feet. Broadsides were tacked up on tavern walls, abandoned buildings, fences, and packet boats advertising Patch's motto, "Some things can be done as well as others."

Winter was already setting in on that November 13, but Sam's fame had spread far, and despite the short notice, crowds began to gather. Schooners made special runs from Canada and Oswego, and hundreds of people made the long, cold trek over difficult roads from Buffalo, Canandaigua, and Batavia. Farmers packed up their families and made their way into the village.

On the day of the jump, Sam climbed the rope ladder to the top of the platform, took a last drink to ward off the November chill and after a lengthy speech to the thousands of people crowding both banks of the river, he leaped into the water. Sam somehow lost his balance and rather than cutting through the water like a knife, he hit the water sideways with a smack.

Sam never surfaced and the crowds' silence turned to mumbles of fear, then speculation that he must have swum to a cave nearby. Trollers patrolled the river all night, their torches casting an eery light on the water. But Sam's body was not found until the following spring near the mouth of the river. He was buried nearby at the Charlotte Cemetery; but those who were there when he jumped could never bury him, for the guilt they felt in encouraging Sam's jump was deepened by the admonitions of the clergy in numerous fiery sermons. More than a century and a half later, Sam Patch and his foolish jump for idle amusement is remembered.

CHURCHES IN THE WILDERNESS

Speaking in 1847 at the first Pioneer Festival, William Alexander said of the pioneer men who established the city, "They were men regardful of religion and its institutions. Their first work was to set up an altar in the wilderness. When sixteen settlers joined together in 1815 to establish the First Presbyterian Church, the first church in Rochester, the population was so sparse that the congregants had to be gathered from "the Ridge in the town of Gates and from the eastern part of the town of Brighton." But it grew rapidly and by 1828, the congregation numbered four and five hundred. When Rev. Charles Finney, the great evangelist, spoke there during the revival of the 1830s, their church south of the courthouse was packed so tightly that many were concerned about the strength of the building to hold them.

In 1817, Nathaniel Rochester had helped to establish St. Luke's Episcopal Church, the Society of Friends organized the same year, the Zion African Church in 1835, an African Methodist Episcopal Church in 1837, and a German Evangelical Lutheran Church (that a few generations later, introduced the Christmas tree to Rochester) in 1835. By 1838 there were twenty-two churches representing nine denominations in the city.

EDUCATION IN A PIONEER CITY

Schools were just as important, for few doubted that the best preparation for life for their children was a strong education. The churches organized the first Sabbath schools. In 1818 St. Lukes Episcopal Church opened the first Sabbath school with only thirty students. The next year there were 120 students. By 1823 six protestant Sabbath schools were open. By 1836, 2,554 students attended Catholic and Protestant schools run by twenty churches. Schools were open only in the summer.

District schools began earlier. Children on the east side of the river attended the first school in Enos Stone's barn near Main Street in 1813. Students on the west side met at Jehiel Barnard's tailor and clothing shop on the corner of Buffalo (West Main) and Carroll (State) streets. When fifteen students registered at the school over the tailor shop; a one-story, eighteen by twenty-four foot school was built on Fitzhugh Street in 1813. The rapid growth of Frankfort required the construction of a second school at Mill and Platt streets in 1815. As the population continued to grow the first school on Fitzhugh Street was twice enlarged before being replaced by a brick building.

Private schools also taught students. In 1830, the Rochester Female Academy on South Fitzhugh Street was organized to give young women "thorough mental discipline and a finished solid education." Another one hundred women attended Miss Seward's Female Seminary established in 1833 in the United States Hotel. Women were taught metaphysics, mathematics, history, botany, elocution, natural science, music, and art.

By 1838, there were thirteen common school districts, twenty Sabbath schools, and several private schools. In 1827 a high school was organized becoming the county's third high school to organize after Wheatland and Henrietta.

By 1853, when the state organized the public school system, every child was offered a free public education and the number of private and Sabbath schools dwindled. In 1850 the University of Rochester opened.

POVERTY IN THE GROWING VILLAGE

Despite the availability of employment opportunities, poverty grew with the population; so in 1822 the Rochester Female Charitable Society organized. Many of the new arrivals to the village were too old or ill or disabled to work. The Society divided the village into sections and a member visited poor families every month providing food, loaning clothing and bedding, helping to find jobs, referring the needy to other sources, and supplying needy children with schoolbooks and paper.

Much of the poverty was rooted in alcohol. Excessive drinking, particularly after the construction of the Erie Canal began, became the focus of complaint by those who observed the ranks of the poor increasing. The first public temperance meeting in Rochester was held on July 21, 1828, after the statewide mailing campaign and a series of newspaper editorials in the *Rochester Observer* awakened citizens to the evils of intemperance. Liquor licenses were for a while seldom given, but when a movement began to grant the licenses more freely, Rochester's first mayor, Jonathan Child, resigned rather than grant the licenses. The temperance movement grew strong and was the focus of many revivals in the 1830s. Though it was nearly laid aside during the antislavery movement in the 1850s, it resurfaced strongly again after the Civil War.

In 1826 the county opened a poorhouse capable of housing seventy-five to one hundred residents, but it quickly became overcrowded. Some people complained about the newly-arrived Irish immigrants, many of whom entered the poorhouse.

If the poor were not too ill or old, the men worked in the fields or in the wood shop. The women and older girls helped with cooking, cleaning, and child care. Younger boys and girls attended school.

An orphan asylum opened on Corn Hill in 1837. Five years later the Catholics opened an orphanage also for some children, it was delinquency rather than poverty that created a need for institutional care. In 1849, the Western House of Refuge was built to discipline young boys in the proper ways of behavior.

The epidemics that periodically struck Rochester were more deadly among the poor. The news-

papers followed the spread of the epidemics of smallpox and cholera which spread even faster after the canal hastened travel. Epidemics spread through Rochester in 1832, 1834, 1849, and 1852. Campaigns to drain swamps and cesspools and to build sewers later helped to curb the epidemics.

British Army Capt. Basil Hall and his wife visited the rapidly growing village of Rochester in 1827 as the guest of Gideon Granger. Granger took the Halls on a tour. They stopped at the Main (Upper) Falls, watched the canal boats cross the recently opened aqueduct over the river, and viewed some of the beautiful mansions built by Nathaniel Rochester, Everard Peck, and several wealthy millers. Like other visitors to the village including Nathaniel Hawthorne, the Halls made notes on the sites and their impressions; but more than that, Captain Hall made drawings, which in an age without cameras, helped to preserve accurate portraits of the village in 1827. He made this drawing of the Court House Square from the second floor window of the Ensworth Tavern using a camera lucida, a box containing mirrors and lenses that projected an image upon which Hall could trace an accurate portrait. Both the Presbyterian Church and the steeple of St. Luke's are visible behind the courthouse.
From the Rochester Public Library

Abelard Reynolds, the village's first postmaster, established the first post office in 1812 in his home on the One Hundred Acre Tract. He conducted his saddlery from the same building. In 1828, Reynolds built The Arcade on this site, the most expensive building west of Albany. The high narrow windows on the storefronts were later replaced by large plate glass windows. The four-story building fronted Main Street for 175 feet. An observatory on the roof gave a view of the city, countryside, and distant Lake Ontario. The walls of the Arcade Hall were decorated with paintings of the Genesee River Falls and Niagara Falls. Skylights, large windows, and gas lights gave plenty of light. One newspaper article said, "The concentration of so many places of business, make it a place of public resort, and during all hours, from dawn to late at night, it is thronged with people, giving an air of cheerful bustle and activity." Doors at the back of the Arcade led to Corinthian Hall on Exchange Place.
From the Rochester Historical Society and the Rochester Public Library

The new public market built after the Main Street Bridge fire of 1834 destroyed the earlier market. The public market was so popular that when the first public market was destroyed, shoppers continued to buy on the burned-out site. The new building faced Front and Market streets with its back to the Genesee River.
From Sketches of Rochester by Henry O'Reilley, 1838

Upon close examination, this undated photograph of Buffalo Street (Main Street West) from Graves to Aqueduct (No. 5 to 17) gives fine details about the store, activities, and dress of Rochester's people and the attractions that merchants used for their customers. Signs on every story advertise agricultural tools, hot air furnaces, house paint, wallpaper, tin, copper, and iron work, bedstead rooms and even teas, coffees, and spices imported and ground by the Van Zandt Brothers. Notice the rooster weather vane on the right of the building numbered 17. An oversized shotgun stands out from the center of the same building like a flag pole. Only the shadow to its left makes us aware of the rifle's outline. Notice the short length of horsecar tracks in the foreground. The streets are crowded with merchandise and men dressed in suit coats; and though a few young boys are visible, not one woman is seen in this photograph from around the 1860s.
From the Rochester Public Library

The Blossom Hotel on Main Street offered one of the finest menus in the city. It was the site of the first gathering of the Pioneer Society of Western New York in October of 1847.
From the 1847 Rochester City Directory

The Farmer's Hotel at the corner of Main and Elm streets was like the farmers' taverns noted by Nathaniel Hawthorne when he visited Rochester in the fall of 1830. He described them as cheap, homely, and comfortable.
Drawing from Sketches of Rochester by Henry O'Reilly, 1838

The Eagle Tavern at the corner of Buffalo (West Main) and State streets on the present site of the Power's Building. From Sketches of Rochester by Henry O'Reilly, 1838

Early visitors to Rochester viewed the 96-foot-high falls, often comparing them to Niagara Falls. Pioneers noted that the falls were much more beautiful before the mills siphoned off much of the water.
From Sketches of Rochester *by Henry O'Reilley*

Men working inside the Boughton and Chase Shingle Factory. Crippling accidents were common among these exposed belts, pulleys, saw blades, and water-wheels. Waterpowered mills required large buildings with high ceilings to ac-commodate the belts. When steam began to be used, the mills required less space and could be built lower and away from the river.
From the Office of the City Historian

In 1856 the Genesee Suspension Bridge replaced the wooden single arch bridge built over the river gorge at Carthage in 1819.
From the Office of the City Historian

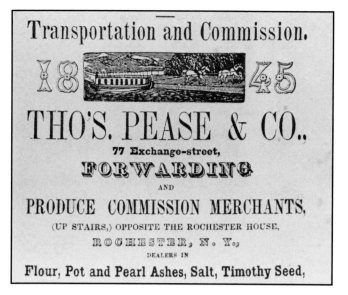

LAKE ONTARIO.

1845. 1845.

THE STEAMER AMERICA,

CAPT. HENRY TWOHY,

Will leave the Port of Rochester, every Monday, Wednesday and Friday, at 9 o'clock, A. M.

For Cobourg, Port Hope, Toronto, and Hamilton.

☞ Passengers for Kingston, will, by leaving on the above mornings, reach Kingston in 12 hours, in time to take Morning Boat for Montreal. The America will meet the Royal Mail Steamer at Cobourg, for Kingston.

Fare to Kingston, --- Cabin,	$4 00		Fare to Toronto, --- Cabin,	$4 00
" Deck,	2 00		" Deck,	2 00
Fare to Hamilton, --- Cabin,	4 00		Fare to Cobourg, --- Cabin,	3 00
" Deck,	1 00		" Deck,	1 50

For further information, apply to J. L. ELWOOD, Esq., 67 Exchange-Street, or WILLIAM NESBITT, Agent.

Lake Ontario offered shippers an outlet to the Canadian and European markets and tourists and travelers found convenient and speedy travel on board the many steamers that plied the lake. Many immigrants traveled from Canada to Rochester through the Port of Rochester. In 1845, the steamer America informed travelers of its schedule.
From the 1845 Rochester City Directory

Transportation and Commission.

18 45

THO'S. PEASE & CO.,

77 Exchange-street,

FORWARDING

AND

PRODUCE COMMISSION MERCHANTS,

(UP STAIRS,) OPPOSITE THE ROCHESTER HOUSE,

ROCHESTER, N. Y.,

DEALERS IN

Flour, Pot and Pearl Ashes, Salt, Timothy Seed,

Forwarders loaded, unloaded, stored, and transported products shipped in the Genesee country. They helped to make connections between canal, lake, and land shippers. The list of products: flour, pot and pearl ash, salt, and timothy seeds emphasized the youth of the Rochester area in 1845 when this advertisement appeared in the Rochester City Directory

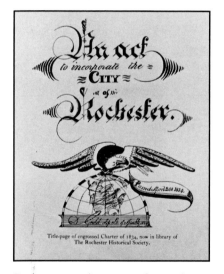

Title-page of engrossed Charter of 1834, now in library of The Rochester Historical Society.

Rochester was incorporated as a city on April 28, 1834. When it incorporated it included other settlements such as Frankfort, the two hundred acre westside tract bordering on Rochester's north side and owned by Matthew and Francis Brown, the eighty acre east-side tract owned by Elisha Johnson and Orson Seymour, and the original west-side One Hundred Acre Tract. The 1,012-acre city of Rochester had a population of 12,252. Jonathan Child, Nathaniel Rochester's son-in-law, was elected as the city's first mayor. This is the original title page of the Charter of 1834.
From the Rochester Historical Society and The Rochester Public Library

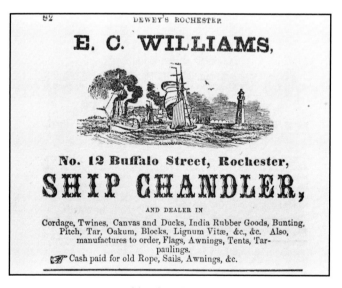

DEWEY'S ROCHESTER

E. C. WILLIAMS,

No. 12 Buffalo Street, Rochester,

SHIP CHANDLER,

AND DEALER IN

Cordage, Twines, Canvas and Ducks, India Rubber Goods, Bunting, Pitch, Tar, Oakum, Blocks, Lignum Vitæ, &c., &c. Also, manufactures to order, Flags, Awnings, Tents, Tarpaulings.
☞ Cash paid for old Rope, Sails, Awnings, &c.

This advertisement for a ship chandler appeared in the Rochester City Directory in 1853. There were many industries that built lake ships or canal boats or in some other way conducted business in shipping.

The first thirty-two mayors of Rochester are identified in this photograph from the Rochester Public Library by their number as:

1. Jonathan Child
2. Jacob Gould
3. Abraham M. Schermerhorn
4. Thomas Kempshall
5. Elisha Johnson
6. Thomas H. Rochester
7. Samuel Andrews
8. Elijah F. Smith
9. Charles J. Hill
10. Isaac Hill
11. John Allen
12. William Pitkin
13. John B. Elwood
14. Joseph Field
15. Levi A. Ward
16. Samuel Richardson
17. Nicholas Paine
18. Hamlin Stillwell
19. John Williams
20. Maltby Strong
21. Charles J. Hayden
22. Rufus Keeler
23. Charles Clark
24. Samuel W. D. Moore
25. Hamlet D. Scrantom
26. John C. Nash
27. Michael Filon
28. Nehemiah C. Bradstreet
29. James Brackett
30. Daniel D. T. Moore
31. Henry L. Fish
32. Edward Meigs Smith

The Western House of Refuge was built by the state for unruly boys in the north-western part of the present Rochester. The site later became Exposition Park, now Edgerton Park. The institution is now the State Industrial School at Industry, New York.
From the Rochester Public Library

The Rev. Charles G. Finney gave sermons in Rochester several times between 1830 and 1855. The fiery sermons delivered by him and numerous tent revival ministers gave upstate New York the name "the burned-over district." Idle amusement, circuses, and daring stunts were criticized, especially the fatal leap of Sam Patch. Those who attended his feat were harshly criticized as having helped to encourage a suicide. By 1838, historian Henry O'Reilly reported that there were no circuses or theatres. Temperance societies, Bible Tract societies, anti-slavery societies, and many other movements were energized by these great revivals and the lessons of the revivals were long-lasting.
From the City Historian's Office

MISS SEWARD'S FEMALE SEMINARY.
In Alexander-street, near the east line of the City of Rochester. See account.

Drawing from Sketches of Rochester *by Henry O'Reilly, 1838*

Broadsides advertising the last jump of the season for daredevil Sam Patch, were posted in packet boats and on fences and tavern walls. Sam's last jump was truly the last.
Broadside from the Rochester Historical Society and the Rochester Public Library

HIGHER YET!
Sam's Last Jump.
"Some things can be done as well as others."

There's no   Mistake in

SAM PATCH.

OF the truth of this he will endeavour to convince the good people of Rochester and its vicinity, next
Friday, Nov. 13, at 2 o'clock P.M.
1829

ROCHESTER FEMALE SEMINARY — Miss J. H. Jones, principal, 1838.

A section of Fitzhugh-street, showing the above Seminary on the left side of the picture, shaded by trees. The building on the right represents a store which has been inserted in some of the newly-constructed dwellings, as well as public buildings. The centre building serves as a representative of the greater portion of the substantial brick or stone dwellings of our citizens.

Drawing from Sketches of Rochester *by Henry O'Reilly, 1838*

Sam Patch made his second jump from this platform that raised the height of the leap to 125 feet. The platform was built in the middle of Brown's Island at the Main (Upper) Falls. Thousands of people crowded the banks on both sides of the river when Patch made his fatal leap on Friday the 13th, 1829. People who came to see him jump were harshly criticized by many ministers for encouraging a fool-hardy jump.
From an engraving by B. Cheney published in the Rochester Gem and Amulet *in 1829; from the Rochester Historical Society and the Rochester Public Library*

When the circus came to town, people traveled from small towns and the countryside to see the acrobats, animals, and sideshows. Newspapers reported the acts in detail and decided if the acts were educational or moral enough to be patronized. After the Civil War, several circuses came to Rochester every summer on a Syracuse, Rochester, and Buffalo circuit. Detail from Robinson's lithograph of Rochester in 1868; Office of the City Historian and the Genesee Country Museum

B. MINGES,

UNDERTAKER, NO. 120 MAIN STREET,
ROCHESTER, N.Y.

Announces to his friends, and the public generally, that he is prepared to attend to all calls on funeral occasions. He will also furnish Hearse and Carriages at all times, if desired. A large assortment of READY-MADE COFFINS, SHROUDS and Trimmings kept constantly on hand. Mr. MINGES flatters himself that he is the owner of the best Hearse west of the city of New York.

The Rochester Museum in 1844 advertised in the City Directory. The museum was considered educational and therefore acceptable amusement. Most of its collection was wax figures.
From the Office of the City Historian

The Rev. Thomas James declared himself free because he lived in Canada before moving to Rochester. He helped to found the African Methodist Episcopal Zion Church and was active on the underground railroad.
From the Monroe County Historian

ROCHESTER MUSEUM,

ENTRANCE,
No. 16, Exchange-street,
JUSTIN R. BISHOP,
PROPRIETOR.

THIS establishment contains upwards of *One Hundred Thousand* rare and interesting Curiosities, collected from every quarter of the globe.

Open every day and evening.

☞ Admittance, 25 cents; children, half price. ☜

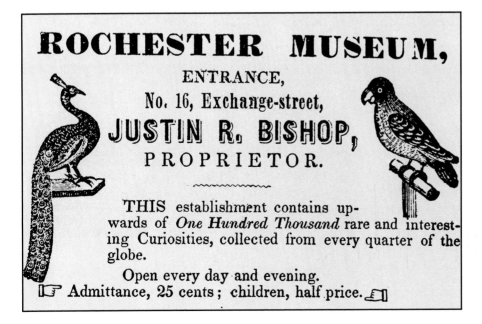

Epidemics periodically swept through Rochester killing scores of people. Death was common, especially among children under five. Minges Undertaking business was one of several undertakers advertised in the Rochester City Directory.

Chapter Four

William Reynolds rented Corinthian Hall
to abolitionists who flew their flag from
the roof of the building. The flag, bearing
the antislavery motto "No Compromise
With Slaveholders," angered many citizens who feared that the nation was
being brought closer to war by such uncompromising attitudes. Reynolds was an
abolitionist, but he agreed to city aldermen's request to forbid the evening use of
the hall by abolitionists in order to prevent riots that threatened the peace of the
city in 1861. William Reynolds was the
son of Abelard Reynolds, the city's first
postmaster and the owner of Reynolds'
Arcade. Reynolds purchased the books of
the old Rochester Athenaeum and opened
Reynolds' Library on Spring Street. That
collection became a part of the Rochester
Public Library when it accepted Reynolds'
Library.
From the Rochester Public Library

ROCHESTER DURING THE CIVIL WAR

AN IRREPRESSIBLE CONFLICT

The issue of slavery was the common thread running through all of the various political, economic, and social causes of the Civil War. Rochester was the heart of much abolitionist activity. The honorable Henry Wilson, a U.S. Senator from Massachusetts, told a large abolitionist audience at Corinthian Hall in 1855 that:

> Twenty years ago the anti-slavery movement was in its infancy . . . . Now it is strong and grown to be a giant. Its followers are counted by hundreds of thousands, and it is now a majority in the House of Representatives, and is fast getting control of the Senate.

The Fugitive Slave Act of 1850 charged the abolitionist movement with new energy and it gained members and supporters who had been disinterested in the slavery issue earlier. The act required everyone to assist in the return of slaves to their masters. No longer could someone be uninvolved. But resistance to the Fugitive Slave Act was widespread. Some judges, marshals, and administrators joined abolitionists.

The Fugitive Slave Act more than quadrupled the traffic through Rochester along the long-established underground railroad. A few abolitionists even penetrated the South preaching freedom and inspiring insurrections; and slaves began to escape to freedom by the hundreds.

Because of the South's renewed efforts to reclaim its slaves, many blacks who had lived free for years in Rochester were forced to flee. Dr. John Jenkins, the city's only black doctor, fled after living freely in Rochester for seventeen years.

The freedom of many slaves like Frederick Douglass was purchased by friends and abolitionists. Free slaves also traveled the country on speaking tours soliciting money to free their families. Austin Steward was declared free by an abolitionist lawyer when his master unlawfully hired him out. He became Rochester's first black grocer. The Reverend Thomas James considered himself free because he had crossed the border into Canada, returning later to find employment in Rochesterville.

The repeal of the Missouri Compromise of 1854 was meant to defuse the slavery issue by allowing states to choose whether they would join the Union as slave or free states. Instead it created a national tension as proslavery and antislavery settlers rushed into Kansas and Missouri to push the vote in their own favor. Missouri was in turmoil and Kansas was in open civil war. The abolitionist movement grew in intensity. When the Missouri Compromise was first repealed, a hurried meeting was called at City Hall in Rochester to protest the reopening of the slavery question. The editor of the *Rochester Daily Union* hoped that a large crowd would attend because, he wrote, "prompt and decided remonstrance may yet avert . . . the danger to the peace of this country."

When the people of Rochester heard the decision of the Supreme Court in the Dred Scott case on March 6, 1857, antislavery supporters again crowded into City Hall to denounce it. The court ruled that Dred Scott was not a U.S. citizen and therefore could not bring suit in court. Further, the Missouri Compromise under which Dred Scott claimed his freedom, was declared unconstitutional. Though the ruling had no direct effect on other blacks, the precedent was set for the lower courts: blacks were not citizens and could not sue in court.

There were 139 attendants at the City Hall meeting as attorney John Chumasero, himself an aspirant to the Supreme Court, spoke in a fiery tone. He called for judges and lawyers to ignore the Fugitive Slave Laws which he considered unenforceable. He challenged the audience "to talk of resistance, and (he) would even name revolution. God forefend that they should resort to arms—the ballot box would do. From there we could send forth to our Southern tyrants the indignant voice of the American people."

The *Union and Advertiser* describes the crowd as "original wool-dyed abolitionists, now prominent members of the Republican party, and no longer of reputation."

The *Rochester Daily Democrat* reported that the Supreme Court decision did not disappoint people as much as it offended them with its intense proslavery views.

Frederick Douglass wrote in his abolitionist newspaper, the *North Star*, that the "decision was an open, glaring, and scandalous tissue of lies . . . ."

The Fugitive Slave Act of 1850, the repeal of the Missouri Compromise in 1854 and the Dred Scott decision in 1857, all combined to agitate abolitionists in Rochester. They believed that now that the slaveholders held the executive office under James Buchanan and had the sympathy of the highest court in the land, political moves would be futile. Violence and civil war would be the next step toward the abolition of slavery.

William Henry Seward of Auburn, Lincoln's main contender for the 1860 Republican presidential nomination, said in a speech in 1858 in Rochester that the Dred Scott decision made civil war inevitable and that the slavery issue was now an "irrepressible conflict."

JOHN BROWN IN ROCHESTER

John Brown was a major instigator in the violence in bloody Kansas, and though that state was distant from Rochester, the issue of slavery's extension was at the heart of the local abolitionist movement. When John Brown and his followers fought in Kansas against proslavery settlers, Susan B. Anthony's brothers Merrit and Daniel were

with him in Kansas and Brown was a frequent visitor to the Rochester homes of the Anthonys and Frederick Douglass. On one visit to Rochester, Brown recruited Shields Green, a clothes cleaner who lived on Spring Street. Green was hanged for his part in the attack on the arsenal at Harper's Ferry, Virginia; but David Cunningham, whose obituary claimed that he too was with Brown, died of typhus in Rochester in 1865.

When Brown was captured by troops in Virginia, papers were found in his carpetbag that implicated Frederick Douglass. A warrant was issued for Douglass' arrest, but a sympathetic telegrapher informed Douglass and on a horse loaned by Henry Selden, Douglass made his way to the ferry on Lake Ontario where he escaped to Canada.

Douglass said that he had heard Brown speak of the attack on numerous occasions and that Brown spoke tirelessly of a mountain fortress where blacks could live free. But Douglass never planned to participate in the attack.

Some sympathetic Rochester abolitionists raised money to try to help Brown escape from prison, but he was so heavily guarded that his rescue was never attempted. On the day that he was hanged a few hundred devout abolitionists, Susan B. Anthony and the Unitarian minister Rev. Parker Pillsbury among them, stood vigil at City Hall.

Brown had become an American legend and by the outbreak of the Civil War, abolitionist sentiments had penetrated the fabric of everyday life in Rochester. In 1861, three years after John Brown's death, three black chimney sweeps sat on the roof of City Hall and sang "John Brown's Body" before disappearing into the chimneys.

THE GROWING CONFLICT

Antislavery activists became more vocal and the success of their movement created a backlash among people who feared that the South would secede from the Union and that the country would engage in civil war. A *Union and Advertiser* editor complained:

The peace of the Union and the business interests of the country should no longer suffer from the cause of a few fanatics . . . (mechanics and laborers) are beginning to realize in Rochester and elsewhere that secession talk is depressing business and construction.

As the issue of slavery became more intense, local abolitionists held more frequent meetings in order to offset the proslavery sentiment that they saw becoming stronger. In 1858, a meeting at City

Hall in Rochester broke into violence when a mob objected to Susan B. Anthony calling the meeting to order. The mob felt that as a woman she did not belong on a public platform. The *Union and Advertiser* charged that Douglass arranged this violence as a publicity tactic, but Douglass criticized the paper and claimed she had a right to speak.

Through speeches and his newspaper Frederick Douglass had a strong influence on an international audience. Even though his speeches were described as incendiary, he did not hold the uncompromising attitude of Susan B. Anthony and the others who signed a resolution denouncing Southerners as criminals with no rights to life, liberty, or the pursuit of happiness. Douglass often focused his antislavery attacks on slaveholding rather than on the slaveholder.

In 1860, in the month in which Southern states began to secede, the abolitionists held a four-day meeting in Rochester. Some people complained about the abolitionist flag waving from the top of the Corinthian Hall. It displayed the motto, "No compromise with slaveholders."

On the first day of the meeting, Elizabeth Cady Stanton opened the meeting before nearly five hundred people. One hundred entered the Hall before it was apparent that not all of the attendants were abolitionists.

The audience was urged to resist the Fugitive Slave Act, but instead the people continuously cheered and applauded the government's conciliatory stance toward the South, effectively preventing Susan B. Anthony from conducting any business. In an attempt to restore order, Monroe County Sheriff Hiram Smith asked that everyone who was for free speech move to the west side of the hall, but everyone, of course, moved to the west side. Instead of bringing order, there was greater confusion when all left their seats. People began to talk louder to gain control of the meeting, but the police turned down the gas lights to prevent that. Crowds were gathered in the stairwells and many stood outside the hall in Exchange Place. Police escorted Anthony, Douglass, Stanton, and others from the meeting to prevent their injury.

Frightened by the outbreak of violence in their own city, the seventeen town aldermen were called to an emergency meeting.

The *Union and Advertiser* reported:

The opinion (of the aldermen) appears to be that freedom is abused at this time by these abolition agitators. They have availed themselves, under a common right on this occa-

sion, to wound the sensibilities of their fellow citizens and to injure the reputation of our city by contributing to the fire which is consuming the nation.

Evicted from Corinthian Hall, the *Union and Advertiser* reported, the abolitionists "who gather when the storm howls, and stir their caldron, singing their impious songs in celebration of the mischief . . . have had their run of this city for three days, and ended their raid on the peace of society at the African Church (Zion African Methodist Episcopal) last night."

THE CIVIL WAR

On the eve of the election, the *Democrat and Chronicle* urged Rochester citizens to vote for Lincoln and assured its readers that the South would not secede if Lincoln were elected.

The following day the paper reported that a majority of the votes cast in the city were cast for Lincoln. Every state in the north voted for Lincoln. In the months that followed, Rochester's citizens watched tensely as Southern states began to secede. When the South captured Fort Sumter, the city waited for news, knowing that war was imminent despite the negotiations in Washington to seek a peaceful solution. The *Democrat and Chronicle* reported "It is the prevailing belief here that a collision is to happen before many days, but on many accounts it is desirable that the blow which inaugurates war shall come from the rebel side."

When the war broke out the paper observed, "On no occasion since the days of the revolution have our citizens undergone the same degree of anxious exciting suspense that characterizes every hour of the day." But Rochesterians were prepared for war by years of growing tension and differing opinions.

From the outbreak of the war, black men in Rochester petitioned to join the armed forces. Blacks had been attached as civilian laborers from the beginning of the war, but they had not been allowed to serve as soldiers to carry arms until Lincoln issued the Emancipation Proclamation which freed the slaves in states in rebellion and allowed the raising of black troops. Three black regiments were raised in New York: the Twentieth, the Twenty-sixth, and the Thirty-first United States Colored Troops. All were raised in early 1864 and discharged in late 1865.

There were black troops raised in other states even before the Emancipation Proclamation was issued, but those troops were not allowed to bear arms. Frederick Douglass, barber James Cleggett, and other black Rochester men gave lectures to raise troops for Massachusetts, Rhode Island, and a few other states. They raised few in Rochester until Douglass' own son enlisted. Abolitionists held Douglass up as the greatest speaker since Henry Clay. His speeches were eloquent, moving, controversial, and inflammatory.

Recruiters struggled to raise enough troops to fill the quotas so a draft was begun. The *Union and Advertiser* thought it was not only fair to have quotas for each county, but that it was just punishment for abolitionists who had led the nation into war. The paper said:

> Had those men who were so terribly valiant during the last presidential election, those men who showed so conclusively that the rebellion could be crushed like an eggshell, those heroes who unflinchingly bore aloft the thousands of dirty lamps which shed such a dismal light on the immense procession of black capes and dirty faces of 1860, ever supposed that their precious carcasses might be forcibly brought within the range of the rebel bullets they then held in such lofty contempt, what an incalculable amount of bloodshed and misery might the nation have escaped.

PEACE AT LONG LAST

The war dragged on for four long years and losses were heavy. When the news of the war's end reached Rochester on April 9, 1865, the *Union and Advertiser* reported to an exhausted city:

> The news of the surrender of Lee was received last night between nine and ten o'clock, and the people of our city became greatly excited by the joy they experienced in the prospect of speedy peace and the restoration of the Union. It being Sunday night and as most of the people had retired to their homes before the news came, it was deemed proper by the mayor to call them up for rejoicing. Notice was sent to the firemen at the several houses that an alarm would be sounded at eleven o'clock. The City Hall bell began to strike and continued to ring for three hours without intermission. The other bells of the city chimed in for a while and helped to swell the notes of victory and peace, and so welcome to every ear. Citizens left their beds by thousands and flocked together in the streets, where they were ad-

vised that Lee had surrendered and the prospect was a speedy peace. The announcement was hailed with cheers and cheer followed cheer for hours.

> Mayor Moore and others addressed the multitude from the steps of Powers' Banking Office, but so great was the confusion that few could hear what was said. Meanwhile bonfires began to blaze in the streets and rockets rent the air. Guns and pistols, everything that would make noise was brought out and put into requisition. For the want of other material a barrel of kerosene or refined petroleum was burned at the corner of State and Buffalo Streets and made a brilliant bonfire. Cannon were at length brought out and fired in the streets and helped to increase the noise that everybody was striving to make louder still. For an impromptu celebration it was a "big thing." The rain began to descend, but it did not check the ardor of those who had enlisted for the night, and it must have been well toward daybreak before the last man left the field to rest. Good feeling was apparent, and all had a hope that a sanguinary civil contest was at an end.

THE ASSASSINATION OF THE PRESIDENT

On April 27, 1865, at 3:30 in the morning the New York Central Depot was already crowded with thousands of men, women and children gathered to see the funeral train, Dean Richmond, that carried the remains of assassinated President Abraham Lincoln.

The depot was draped in solemn colors as the people waited in the darkness, when the pilot train arrived announcing the approach of the funeral train. The pilot train, engine No. 79, was decorated with black flowers. David Upton, the master mechanic of Rochester's NYCRR, was aboard Lincoln's funeral train as he had been when the train carried Lincoln through Rochester in 1861 on his way to the inauguration. The Dean Richmond, named in honor of the New York Central president, carried a crepe-trimmed portrait of the fallen president on its front. American flags were placed around the portrait and black and white roses bordered it. Hundreds of Rochester women helped Mrs. Upton to decorate the train and depot.

The Fifty-fourth Regiment, the National Guard, the Veterans Reserve Corps, the invalid Soldiers at the hospital, the Gray's Battery, and the Union Blues formed lines at the depot to officially receive the train of nine cars. City police formed a line to keep back the crowd. As the train rolled to a stop the minute guns fired a salute. The church bells tolled slowly and deeply from the arrival of the train until it passed out of the city fifteen minutes later. A few women boarded the train to view the body before it moved on in the night towards Buffalo. The Common Council and many private citizens followed the funeral train.

The *Union & Advertiser* observed on April 27, 1865, "What rapid transition from rejoicing of the most excited and jubilant character to feelings of the profoundest melancholy pervading the public heart, to the exhibition of a country's sorrow."

Frederick Douglass (1817-1895) earned an international reputation as an abolitionist. He began publishing his abolitionist newspaper, the North Star *(later called* Frederick Douglass' Paper), *in 1847 in Rochester. He worked closely with Susan B. Anthony to end slavery and later to win voting rights for blacks and women. He was one of the nation's most eloquent and incendiary antislavery speakers. He met with presidents and was appointed as ambassador to Haiti after the Civil War. Douglass was born into slavery. His freedom was purchased by an antislavery society in England. He was honored in Rochester after his death when a life-size statue of him was erected at St. Paul Street and Central Avenue. His son Charles was used as a model. The statue was later moved and now overlooks the Highland Bowl at Highland Park near his former home. Douglass died in Washington, D.C., in 1895. His body was brought to Rochester for burial and now rests at Mount Hope Cemetery.*
From the Rochester Public Library

Austin Steward, a slave, declared himself free in 1815 when his master hired him out, an act many jurists viewed as a circumvention of a 1785 New York State law that forbade the sale of slaves. Abolitionists helped Steward to open a grocery and butcher shop on the site of the Holiday Inn Downtown on Main Street next to the river. Steward became a trustee of the African Methodist Episcopal Church and often held antislavery and suffrage meetings. Steward spent a decade in Canada in an attempt to establish Wilberforce, a black colony where runaway slaves could live freely. Steward published his autobiography, Austin Steward: Twenty-two Years a Slave and Forty Years a Free Man, in 1851. This steel engraving is from the frontispiece of that book in the Rochester Public Library.

The arrest of John Brown and Shields Green at Harper's Ferry as it appeared in this engraving from Frank Leslie's Illustrated Weekly in 1859.
From the Office of the City Historian

John Brown visited several times in Rochester with Susan B. Anthony and Frederick Douglass. Anthony's brothers fought with Brown in the bloody Kansas wars. Brown spoke to Douglass about his plans to attack Harper's Ferry Arsenal and he recruited Shields Green, a free black clothes cleaner from Rochester, to go with him. Green was hanged for his part in the attack and Douglass was warned by a sympathetic telegrapher that a warrant had been issued for his arrest after papers implicating his involvement were found in Brown's carpetbag. John Brown became an American legend after he was hanged in 1859. In 1861 three black chimney sweeps sat on the roof of City Hall and sang "John Brown's Body" before disappearing into the chimneys.
From an engraving in Frank Leslie's Illustrated Weekly, Nov. 19, 1859 at the Rochester Public Library

Governor Wise appears in this engraving from Frank Leslie's Illustrated Weekly in 1859, pulling Frederick Douglass and others into Virginia where he could crush the abolitionist movement after their involvement in the attack on Harper's Ferry.
From the Office of the City Historian

52

Myron Holley (1779-1841) was a Universalist and editor of the Rochester Freeman, an abolitionist newspaper that advocated the ballot in a split with the more violent Garrisonian abolitionists. His death in 1841 was a severe blow to the abolitionist movement that intensified over the next two decades.
From the Rochester Public Library

Many abolitionist meetings were held at the Zion African Methodist Episcopal Church at Ford and Spring streets. It was built in 1827, the year New York outlawed slavery. Housewives, laborers, barbers, and hackmen made up many of the abolitionists among the congregants. The church was the site of many antislavery meetings.
From the Rochester Public Library

In 1858, William Henry Seward, Lincoln's main contender for the 1860 Republican presidential nomination, made a speech at Corinthian Hall that became famous when he termed the slavery issue, the "irresponsible conflict."
Engraving from Frank Leslie's Illustrated Weekly, *1858; photograph in the Office from the City Historian*

Corinthian Hall, in the Athenaeum Building, was a concert and lecture Hall built by William Reynolds opposite the Reynolds' Arcade across Exchange Place. It appears in this engraving from the Rochester Athenaeum and Mechanics' Association Catalog *from 1866.*
From the Rochester Public Library

Susan B. Anthony learned to be a convincing writer, speaker, and administrator under Elizabeth Cady Stanton (seated). They both devoted their lives to woman's rights and the abolition of slavery. Nei-ther of the women lived to see a national victory for the suffrage movement though many states granted suffrage.
From the Rochester Public Library

Many abolitionist meetings were held here at Corinthian Hall. Banquets, charity fundraisers, and entertainers like the Swedish Nightingale, Jenny Lind, performed at this Hall. Speakers like Louis Aggaziz, Wendell Phillips, Susan B. Anthony, Elizabeth Cady Staton, and Frederick Douglass spoke here. This engraving appeared in the Illustrated American Supplement, T. W. Strong, in September of 1851, showing a banquet at the New York State Fair in 1851.

The Waverly Hotel at the corner of State Street and Central Avenue next to the New York Central Railroad was busy with passengers dining and sleeping at the hotel from the time it opened in 1848. Baggage men carried heavy trunks and coaches carried baggage and passengers to and from the station. Departing and arriving trains were announced in the dining area. Mrs. Abraham Lincoln dined at the hotel in 1861 on her way to Niagara Falls for a vacation. She spoke pleasantly with several people before her train departed. The hotel was later named the Savoy Hotel.
From the Rochester Public Library

President-elect Abraham Lincoln was scheduled to arrive at this New York Central Railroad Station in 1861, but an aide, fearing a delay in their trip to Washington, had the train stop at Mill Street just short of the station. Lincoln was scheduled to speak at the Waverly Hotel next to the station (the corner of the hotel is visible in the lower right corner). He did speak briefly from the platform of the train and a young boy scampered up the steps as the train began to move away. President Lincoln came to the city four years later when his funeral train, the Dean Richmond, (named for the president of the NYCRR) passed through the city at 3:00 A.M. on April 27, 1865. Crowds gathered in the darkness to see the funeral train on one of the most solemn occasions in the city's history.
From the Rochester Public Library

Newspapers sold quickly when there was news of the war. Young boys stood on street corners and sold newspapers to anxious families and friends of soldiers far from home. At night boys held lanterns to see by and to be seen by rumbling wagons and passersby. Norman Aylsworth was twelve years old when he was photographed about 1861 selling the Rochester Democrat. Aylsworth was born in 1848 and died in 1882.
From the Rochester Public Library

During all hours, Reynolds' Arcade on Main Street was filled with activity from the many businesses within it. With the post office and the telegraph office, the Arcade was the gathering place of many who were anxious for news from the battlefield. Hiram Sibley made an important contribution to communications in consolidating the telegraphs into the Western Union Telegraph just prior to the Civil War. It greatly aided Civil War generals who needed information quickly. Before the war, women collected money for charity, antislavery, and suffrage movements inside the hall. Several black businesses, like barber shops, were located at this desirable business location. This engraving shows the interior of Reynolds Arcade about 1850.
From the Rochester Public Library

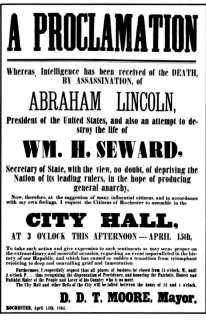

News of the assassination of President Lincoln brought an abrupt end to the joy of peace. The Union & Advertiser observed on April 27, 1865, "What rapid transition from rejoicing of the most excited and jubilant character to feelings of the profoundest melancholy pervading the public heart, to the exhibition of a country's sorrow." Mayor D. D. T. Moore issued one of the most stirring mayoral proclamations in the city's history. Thousands of people gathered in the early morning darkness on April 27 at the New York Central Railroad Station on State Street to pay their respects to the funeral train of their slain president.
From the Rochester Historical Society and the Rochester Public Library

News of General Robert E. Lee's surrender at Appomatox reached Rochester about 9:00 P.M. on Sunday, April 9, 1865. Church bells and fire bells rang throughout the city summoning thousands of people from their beds to the streets of downtown where they heard the news. The City Hall bell began to toll and continued without intermission for three hours. Mayor D. D. T. Moore spoke from the steps of the Powers Banking Office at the Four Corners where construction of the Powers' Block was about to begin, but there was so much noise he could not be heard. Guns were fired, firecrackers were set off, and cheer followed cheer until well into the morning. A barrel of kerosene was ignited at the corner of State

and Buffalo streets casting a brilliant light on the cheering crowd. The rain began to fall, but that did not dampen the spirits of the crowd, for a cannon was rolled into the streets and fired repeatedly 'til near daybreak. Farmers learned of the end of the war the next day when horseback riders shouted, "Peace!" as they galloped down the country roads. Crowds gathered outside of Reynolds' Arcade to receive news from the Western Union Telegraph Office and newspapers sold out quickly in the streets.
From the Rochester Public Library

Carriages and streetcars passed under the Victory Arch built across Main Street at the corner of State Street for the Fourth of July, 1865. Edward A. Frost, the nurseryman, financed the arch in celebration of freedom, independence, and peace, hardwon by the heroes named and the men under them. Notice the horsecar tracks cutting through the macadam street, the paving bricks laid at the crosswalks, and brick gutters at the edge of the street. Gas lamps lighted some of the streets of the city by this date.
From the Rochester Public Library

Chapter Five

Advertisement from the City of Rochester, Illustrated *published by the* Post Express *Printing Company in 1890.*

ROCHESTER MADE MEANS QUALITY

After the Civil War, people turned their attention to private affairs and business and civic projects that had been neglected during the war. The flour industry, though grinding more barrels of flour than earlier, lost dominance as the "Flour City" to western millers. The seed and nursery industries made Rochester the "Flower City" and remained strong until after the turn of the century. Industries like shoes and clothing, already established in Rochester, began to lead among manufacturers. Hundreds of Italian and German immigrants, skilled in needed trades, arrived to support the growing, established businesses, while inventors and creative businessmen opened new opportunities for labor.

THE FLOUR INDUSTRY

Ebenezer (Indian) Allan's early mills had failed, but when Colonel Rochester's son Thomas joined with Harvey Montgomery and other investors to blast out the Rochester Race over the failed Allan Race he was confident that the mill site would be a success. Men from up and down the river joined in the raising of the first mill. This Red Mill, built in 1814, was the first of many built in a few short years. Elisha Ely, Hervey Ely, and Josiah Bissell built their mill on the site of the present Lawyer's Cooperative Publishing Company Building south of the Red Mill, and Joseph Strong's Mills were built on the north side. Benjamin Campbell built his mill near the first aqueduct built over the river in 1823. His majestic home, not far south along the present I-490 remains under the ownership of the Landmark Society of Western New York.

Farther north, Francis and Matthew Brown cut out a raceway at the Main Falls settlement named Frankfort. Just a few years after Brown's Race opened in 1816, there were several mills operating on both sides of the river: the Trip Hammer Mill, the Phoenix Mill, Warham and Whitney, Silas O. Smith, H. P. Smith, Richard Richardson, and the Selye Fire Engine Company. Rochester Gas and Electric Company now generates electricity from the water power of Brown's Race.

On the east side of the river, Elisha Johnson and Orson Seymour built their race from Court Street to Main Street. They began blasting on July 4, 1817. The Johnson and Seymour Race was barely finished when William Atkinson built the Yellow Mill near the Main Street Bridge. Homes and mills were built on the eighty-acre tract owned by Johnson and Seymour. The tail races that once spilled from the Ely's Atkinson Mill on this race are now part of the foundation to the Rochester Gas and Electric substation at Broad Street and South Avenue. Horatio Curtis built his mill just south of the Main Street Bridge. Also on the site of the Riverside Convention Center, Thomas Emerson built the Crescent Mill. The water held back by Johnson's dam at Court Street powered both the Rochester and the Johnson and Seymour races. The mills were already faring well when Johnson donated a piece of his land to accommodate the Erie Canal aqueduct. On October 29, 1822, even before the canal was opened to Albany, the Atkinson and Ely mills on the Johnson and Seymour Raceway shipped the first boat load of Rochester milled flour eastward to Little Falls, New York.

The Johnson and Seymour Race still runs under the Rochester Public Library on South Avenue where it can be seen spilling from the arches in the back of the building into the river below. It was once channeled under Water Street on the present sites of the Riverside Convention Center and the Holiday Inn.

North of the Johnson and Seymour Race, the Third Water Power Tract, built near the present Bausch Bridge, powered mills from a dam, but it did not have the potential of a new settlement, Carthage, built on the east side of the river by the Lower Falls where the mills of Elisha Strong, Heman Norton, and E. Beach prospered. A dam built on the twenty-five foot upper step of the Lower Falls diverted water to power mills on both sides of the river. The lower step of the falls dropped water eighty-five feet, creating a tremendous source of power. Carthage's developer, Elisha Strong of Canandaigua, saw the potential for economic growth based on the combination of water power from the falls and access to lake shipping.

The flour industry prospered for decades before losing the title of the "Flour City" to western millers. In 1827 when the first Rochester *Village Directory* was published, there were ten mills grinding more than two hundred thousand barrels of flour. By the time the city was chartered in 1834, there were twenty-one mills. In its heydey in the 1850s, the Rochester flour industry shipped more than seven hundred thousand barrels of flour world-wide. But times changed. By the end of the 1850s, the flour milling industry had suffered several seasons of wheat blight and it could not compete with the western millers who were nearer to the midwestern fields. Looking for a new market, wheat farmers soon found it in the rising number of breweries.

THE MAKING OF FLOWER CITY

Traveling along the Erie Canal in the summer of 1835, on his first visit to America, George Ellwanger, a German immigrant, wrote:

> In passing through Rochester a halt was made to unload some freight, which gave me an opportunity to inspect the then infant city on the Genesee whose appearance impressed me, especially its luxuriant vegetation and its favorable location for horticultural establishment. The Erie Canal, moreover, made it a highway to the west.

Ellwanger was on his way to Ohio to spend some time with relatives, but he soon returned to Rochester and took charge of Michael Bateham's Rochester Seed Store and Horticultural Repository. He had recently ended a four-year apprenticeship with a leading nurseryman in Stuttgart, Germany.

Rochester was well-suited for the seed and nursery industry. The lake kept the air cool into the spring delaying the planting season until all chance of frost was past. In the fall, it kept the air warm, thus extending the growing season.

The canal was completed just three years after the first nursery opened for business under the ownership of Electus Boardman. In 1833, Asa Rowe opened his nursery, the Monroe Garden and Nursery in Greece by his tavern on Ridge Road near the present Long Pond Road. The canal gave a needed boost to the nursery business.

Before the canal opened in 1825, it took twenty days to ship freight between Buffalo and New York City and the freight charges were one hundred dollars a ton. The canal cut the cost to ten dollars a ton which opened a large western market that needed new seeds and trees. With the faster shipping available, the newer industries in Rochester had a five to eight day lead over the older industries in Albany or Long Island. Not only was speed essential to gaining the market, it was essential to keeping the trees alive and the seeds fresh.

The seed and nursery men did not have an easy time winning the market in Rochester when they first established themselves, however. The flour industry was just beginning to decline as the new industry was beginning, but farmers in the Genesee region only wanted to grow wheat. Naaman Goodsell, who started the first garden seed nursery in 1832 on Buffalo Street, recognized the profitability of the new industry. He said, "the raising of garden seeds for market appears to be entirely overlooked by the farmers of western New York (and) . . . if proper attention were paid to it, few agricultural pursuits would afford a greater profit."

His Rochester Seed Store began to receive orders for trees, shrubs, plants, and seeds and he planted a five-acre nursery garden in order to sell his own stock and to be independent of other nurseries.

Goodsell not only had to wrest the farmer from wheat growing, he had to retrain the farmers, whose habits had been to exhaust the fertility of a farm and to move on to western, more fertile lands. He tried to teach rotation of crops and fertilization, but the farmers were slow to accept it.

Only a few months after Naaman Goodsell went to Flushing, New York, to study the large and successful William Prince Nursery, he opened the Rochester Seed Store. In 1832, he also began a garden nursery on Buffalo Street to begin weaning himself from dependence upon older nurseries elsewhere.

When Electus Boardman opened his nursery in 1822, Asa Rowe had already been selling apple trees at King's Landing since the 1790s. He advertised his Monroe Garden and Nursery in a four-page insert in the Genesee Farmer. His Greece garden grew apples, pears, peaches, grapes, roses, and other plants.

Even though there were many horticultural businesses in the Rochester area, the *Genesee Farmer* reported in 1839 that few were involved in the business. Luther Tucker who published the *Genesee Farmer* was himself involved in flower seeds. William Reynolds and Michael Bateham joined to open the Rochester Seed Store and Horticultural Repository on the former site of Naaman Goodsell's Nursery, this was the business that George Ellwanger managed when he first came to the city.

Asa Rowe was well established by this date and had arranged with Charles Crosman to raise seeds for Rowe on Monroe Avenue. Only ten years later, Crosman was selling thousands of dollars worth of seeds through agents from New York City to Detroit. His seed house became the largest in the world. In 1890 he had over twelve hundred acres in seeds in the Rochester area.

As the new settlements developed in the west, the demand for food and seeds increased, thus raising the prominence of seedsmen in the horticultural industry. Just as the canal helped the nursery industry, the railroad helped the seed industry. There was a great demand for vegetables such as beets, turnips, corn, lettuce, and berries and fruits such as pears, apples, peaches, and plums. The railroad allowed the wide distribution of catalogues and the mail order business grew so large that a business grew up among middlemen, brokers, and lithographers who printed the colored catalogues.

James Vick began to develop his own seeds on Union Street in 1855 because he could not find quality seeds in America. Although Crosman was already selling seeds, Vick imported his from France. In 1866 he bought an old race track in what is now Vick Park A and Vick Park B off East Avenue. He developed the most widely known mail order seed business in America. He had over fifty additional acres planted in seeds in Greece and bulbs in Greece, Irondequoit, and Ogden.

Joseph Harris came to the Rochester area from England as Vick did and he too built a large mail-order business in Gates in 1879. He appealed to

the public's need to be self-sufficient. Too many people, he thought, were raising cash crops, particularly wheat, and depending on that cash to provide everything. Why not, he argued, grow the foods needed? This was an especially appealing argument after the Civil War when the sealable jar made canning possible.

Zerah Burr of Perinton researched and developed several varieties of strawberries, a plant that became very popular in the 1850s. Rawson Harmon of Wheatland developed the Rohan Seed potato and grew Swaar and Spitzenburgh apples.

Even the silkworm industry was tried in the Rochester area. Early in the history of horticulture, farmers were urged to grow mulberry trees to support the profitable silkworm industry, but the industry soon failed and left the farmers lukewarm to the entire horticultural business.

Even though there were many nurserymen and seedsmen who were successful in their own right, it was George Ellwanger and Patrick Barry who made horticulture sucessful. Patrick Barry had worked for the William Prince Nursery that Naaman Goodsell studied in 1832. Barry brought the skill of this nursery to the partnership in 1840 when the two opened the Mount Hope Nursery. They built their reputation on accurate labeling and hardy stock, making strengths from the weaknesses of other nurseries. Lake Ontario's temperate climate gave them an advantage over the Mohawk Valley and New England because the cold weather made the plants hardy enough to survive the demands of the west. They became the leading wholesale and retail business in America. They opened a branch in Toronto in addition to the forty-three-acre Mount Hope Nursery. Even William Prince and Sons, the large nursery in Flushing, bought stock wholesale from Ellwanger and Barry.

Many other nursery and wholesale businesses, some quite large, grew up around Mount Hope Nurseries. William King opened in 1844. Samuel Moulson who ran the old Rochester Nursery on North and Norton streets opened a seed store in 1845. Josiah Bissell and Horace Hooker bought the fifteen-acre nursery of Electus Boardman on East Avenue near Goodman. There was a demand, particularly in the west, for seeds. Flowers, however, were expensive so only the upper class could afford to plant them. One chrysanthemum cost about $1.50, a day's wages for many.

Ellwanger and Barry did not confine their business to their forty-three-acre nursery. They donated fifty shade trees to nearby Mount Hope Cemetery. Not only did the people come on the streetcar to the nursery, they now saw the beautiful trees in the cemetery. People were encouraged to plant them along city streets and in their yards.

The industry began to decline when the west no longer had a great demand for seeds and trees. By the 1870s much of the Ellwanger and Barry's business was in the foreign market. But in their heyday in the 1850s, over half of the nurserymen in the state were in the Rochester area. There were more fruit trees sold in Monroe County than in the rest of America in 1856. There were over one thousand people employed in the nurseries and there was more nursery acreage in Monroe County than in any other county in the state: Alonzo Frost and Company had two hundred and fifty acres in their Genesee Valley Nursery, Ellwanger and Barry had five hundred acres in the Mount Hope Nursery, and Samuel Moulson planted three hundred acres in the old Rochester Nursery. W. J. Mandeville and H. S. King joined in 1878 on East Avenue. Hiram Sibley already had made a fortune in Western Union when he opened a seed business in his nine-story building in Chicago. He employed about five hundred people and owned forty thousand acres in Cayuga County. Seedsmen planted hundreds of acres too.

But it was not only the saturation of the western market that depressed the industry. World War One cut off the supply of stock from England, Germany, and France so that those businesses that were not self-suficient could not survive. Briggs Brothers, began in 1849, failed in 1897 although it continued as a commission house until 1920.

When Vick's was bought out by Burpee Seed Company in 1920, Harris Seeds bought their local acreage. Henry Mapstone bought Crosman in 1925. Harris was bought by the Celanese Corporation in 1979 and bought back in 1987. By 1918, Ellwanger and Barry was closed. They had subdivided their land between South and Highland avenues for 118 homes at a cost of a quarter of a million dollars. Other nurseries followed their lead. Much of Ellwanger and Barry's old Mount Hope Nursery was given to the city in 1888 and is now Highland Park, noted for its beautiful lilacs and flowering trees. A pavilion was erected in the park by the Ellwanger and Barry firm to honor the children of Rochester.

Though the horticultural industry has long since declined, it has had a lasting effect on Rochester. More than most other cities in America Rochester has beautiful parks, streets, and private homes planted amid flowers and flowering trees. Much of the surrounding countryside was planted with acres of orchards and the canning and fruit juice industry became substantial employers. This industry has since declined, but Rochester will always be remembered as the Flower City.

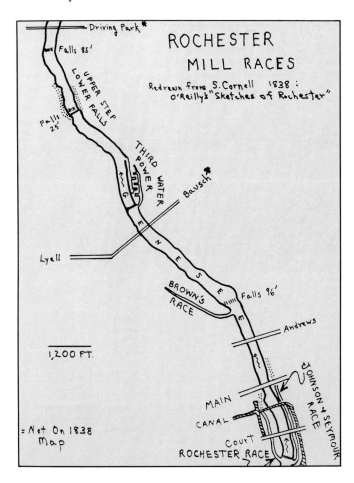

This map of the millraces in Rochester in 1838 shows the power the Genesee River generated in the mills over a short distance. The One Hundred Acre Tract is at the site of the Rochester Race and Main Street on the west side of the river. Frankfort was northward including Brown's Race. On the east side of the river near the present Driving Park Bridge was the village of Carthage and about a quarter of a mile northward on the west side was Hanford's Landing. This map was redrawn by Thomas X. Grasso from Silas Cornell's 1838 map and is in Grasso's collection.

THE SHOE INDUSTRY

Rochester's shoe manufacturing industry dominated for half a century before being eclipsed by the clothing industry and still later by the photographic and photocopier industry. Shoemakers were among the earliest craftsmen, usually setting up shop in their homes. They sometimes doubled as tanners or bought leather from the tanners operating along the Genesee but the Erie Canal gave access to New York City suppliers. They worked with hand tools, cutting, sewing, pegging, and sometimes sending out to home workers some of the finishing work.

With hundreds of newcomers arriving annually, Rochester could support the nearly one hundred shoemakers living here in the mid-1820s, but the individual shoemakers were soon organized into shops where each performed a specialized job. Jesse Hatch was the first shoemaker to hire women in the 1830s to sew uppers. The opening of the Erie Canal made Rochester a provisioning center and its shoemakers found a rich market supplying shoes to thousands of migrants moving west as well as newcomers settling in the growing city. The shipping routes allowed some of Rochester's manufacturers to expand their market to Canada and beyond by lake ships and to the eastern and western markets by canal. The shoe industry followed other industries in using machinery to perform many jobs such as the cutting, sewing, and pegging of shoes. This prompted shoemakers to organize during the Civil War to insure that their jobs were protected. Shops were consolidated and machinery was being introduced and these two factors combined to reduce the number of independent craftsmen employed. In 1863, the first five shoemakers' unions organized and became the Rochester Trades Assembly. Strikes were called against Gould Company in 1871, E. P. Reed in 1875, A. H. Johnson in 1880, and Cox Shoe Company in 1890. The rash of strikes created the need for the organization of the Employers Protective Association.

But in the depression of the mid-1890s, the shoe industry was losing its dominance to the clothing industry. Pioneer shoemakers like Jesse Hatch had seen the shoe industry from its infancy through its decline.

THE CLOTHING INDUSTRY

Jehiel Barnard, the city's first tailor, arrived in 1812 and soon other tailors arrived. In a growing village there was a ready market for custom-made clothing and men's suits cut by the tailor and sewn at home. In little more than a decade, the clothing industry had access to a growing whole-

James Vick (1818-1882) emigrated to America in 1833, arriving in Rochester from New York City in 1837. He worked as writer, editor, then owner of the Genesee Farmer, *a horticultural newspaper. He published the Horticulturist from the estate of Andrew Jackson Downing, the famous landscape architect, and published it in Rochester from 1853 to 1855. Patrick Barry edited the publication. Vick also edited* The Rural Annual and Horticultural Directory *and the* Rural New Yorker. *Vick was not content to write about horticulture. He purchased land on East Avenue at the present Vick Park A and Vick Park B and began to grow seeds, storing them in the attic of his home until his thriving seed business allowed him to move to a four-story building at the corner of State and Market streets. Vick later bought fifty acres in Greece for a seed farm. Vick built his seed business into an international mail order seed business, mailing more that two hundred thousand catalogues in 1872 alone. Vick's business was purchased by Burpee Seed Company in 1920.*
From an engraving in The History of Monroe County *by W. H. McIntosh, at the Rochester Public Library*

sale market through the Erie Canal. Immigrants, particularly German Jews and later Poles, helped to meet the demands for labor created by a growing number of manufacturers and wholesalers like German-born Myer Greentree, Joseph Wile, Sigmund Stettheimer, and Henry Michaels. Most of the shops were small frame buildings on the north end of the Main Street Bridge and adjoining Front Street. Within a small building there was a salesroom, a cutting room, and storage room. Immigrant men, women, and children accepted the tasks of sewing and trimming in their homes and even though sweatshop conditions often developed, the immigrants were anxious to earn badly needed money.

During the Civil War the shops were kept busy filling orders for uniforms, but when the war ended many of the shops sent traveling salesmen on the road to win contracts for the shops that doubled in number in the decade following the war. Stettheimer, McDonnell and Company became the largest partnership while Henry Michaels and Nathan Levi merged in 1868, along with Herman Rosenberg, Jacob Kolb, Nathan Stein, and Levi Adler in 1869. Suits included not only quality, custom-made clothing, but also ready-made clothing which had been long supplied by the industry. Leopold Garson, Simon Hays, and Morris Schwarz met the great demand for ready-made suits in the growing west.

Partnerships were formed and dissolved frequently in the late 1800s. In 1899 Jeremiah Hickey and Jacob Freeman formed a new company. The large Michaels, Stern and Company was formed by the partnership of Henry Michaels, Morley A. Stern and Company with Stein and Adler. The new company manufactured boys' coats and pants. Their installation of water-powered sewing machines in a Mill Street factory led other factories to move to Mill Street thus moving the center of the clothing industry northward.

The depression of the 1870s forced some factories to close or to subcontract for larger firms, but in 1879 the eighteen wholesale clothing manufacturers supported twenty-seven hundred workers, mostly women and children who worked at home.

Moses Hays' necktie factory was expanded by Herman Cohn less than a decade after it was organized in 1869. Using a new process to manufacture buttons from sliced imported vegetable ivory nuts, Moses Shantz built his factory into the largest in the country. Max Lowenthal produced knitted mittens, socks, and mufflers and was quick to adopt the new knitting machinery invented by J. W. Lomb and produced in Rochester.

It was often the reluctance to modernize or accept new business practices that caused the failure of business. Adapting modern business practices, Michaels, Stern and Company; L. Adler Brothers

James Vick's Farm in 1877 in Greece. His nursery was on East Avenue at the present site of Vick Park A and Vick Park B. Vick also owned a fifty acre seed farm in Greece. The flower, seed, and nursery industry grew into a major industry that earned Rochester the name the "Flower City." Flowers and landscaped gardens became common in private yards, even among working families. Many of the nurseries were subdivided into building lots after the decline of the industry. Even today the numerous gardens of the city and county parks as well as private lots show the influence of the flower industry. Engraving from the History of Monroe County *by W. H. McIntosh, 1877, in the Rochester Public Library*

and Company; Stein, Block and Company, and others began to specialize. To better control operations they had moved into larger quarters on St. Paul and Mill Street. This modernization brought some workers reluctantly from their homes into the factories. Anxious to fill contracts, factories hired subcontractors whose hiring of other German, Polish, and Russian homeworkers often created sweatshop conditions that concerned the public health officer. The Knights of Labor found it difficult to tightly organize the clothing industry, but throughout the 1890s the industry struggled to operate during strikes. The Knights of Labor ended the century weakened and the United Garment Workers found organizing equally difficult.

But Emma Goldman, a sixteen-year-old Russian immigrant, campaigned against poor working conditions. She worked at Garson Factory for two months in 1886 before she quit, frustrated by conditions and unable to obtain a raise. She moved to New York City where she became a nationally known anarchist. Meanwhile Rochester's clothing industry earned a reputation for quality clothing world-wide.

In 1912 a particularly violent strike was called by United Garment Workers. In February, when strikers were marching around Clifford Avenue, they noticed factory lights burning. The owner of the factory panicked when strikers beat at the

front and back doors and he fired a rifle into the crowd killing seventeen-year-old Ida Braiman and wounding several others. Police, marching with the strikers, safely ushered the owner away. The strike ended in February, but the peace did not last. It was finally settled in May of 1913. But despite the consolidations, mergers, strikes, and business failures throughout its history, the clothing industry has maintained its reputation for quality.

THE GROWTH OF THE BREWING INDUSTRY

Breweries were among the earliest industries in Rochester. The Aqueduct Spring Brewery is believed to be the first, though no accurate date could be found. By 1824, Reuben Bennett, N. Lyman, and the Rochester Brewery all advertised in the newspapers. Ales were first made in 1837 and lager was introduced in 1850. The demand for lager increased with the growing German population after the Civil War so that the number of companies in the city grew to fifteen by 1890. Many were opened by German immigrants. The taste for lager over ale grew among Americans increasing the production of beer in Rochester to 112,000 barrels by 1878, 146,948 by 1879, and 320,000 barrels by 1889. Rochester be-

Hiram Sibley opened a seed store after he made a fortune with his consolidation of the telegraphs into the Western Union Telegraph Company, headquartered in Rochester.
Engraving from the History of Monroe County *by W. H. McIntosh, 1877 in the Rochester Public Library*

came one of the leading beer producing cities in the country by the 1880s, producing more than its earlier rival—Buffalo.

By 1890, Bartholomay was the largest brewery in the city followed by Rochester, Genesee, and Miller. Sales were about $2,225,000. One million pounds of hops and one and a half million bushels of barley-malt were consumed in the production of beer, creating a demand for the cultivation of hops and barley. The companies used modern equipment and aged their beer in large cellars hewn in the limestone rock below the Upper Falls. Before the mid-1870s brewers drew their water from the springs but water is a critical ingredient in beer, so when fresh Hemlock Lake water became available, the companies believed their product improved owing greatly to the improvement of the water quality.

The growth of the beer industry was not without resistance, though. The temperance movement was growing stronger and the WCTU (Womens' Christian Temperance Union) campaign against the "vile" drink was countered by local beer makers who opened a free bar in 1879 in Reynolds' Arcade.

For generations the temperance movement was strong and growing in Rochester as well as the nation. Finally in January of 1920, the Fourteenth Amendment, prohibiting the making of alcohol for consumption, became effective. Many of the com-

panies closed, but Bartholomay became a dairy and Quality Brewer and American Brewing Company, which became Rochester Food Products, made low-alcohol near beer.

City Health Officer George Goler said Prohibition should greatly reduce the number of alcohol-related deaths, but in fact the drinking of illegally-made poison brew actually increased alcohol-related deaths. Goler wanted neither a repeal nor a modification of the amendment. When asked about the apparent increase in drinking of illegal alcohol, Goler attributed it to a more general freedom of the times.

But public drinking was not to be easily stopped. Police found a three hundred-gallon still in an Ontario Street garage and an electric still in a large building on North Union Street. Eighty-nine barrels of beer made in Oswego were confiscated from the Lehigh Valley Frieght Yard on South Avenue. The barrels were marked "saurkraut" and were to be sold for the Christmas season.

Some deaths occurred from poisoned brews and at least one man was murdered in consequence of his illegal business. The Coast Guard stepped up their guard of the vast Lake Ontario coast line, especially after Ontario, Canada went "wet" in 1927. Smuggled Canadian brew was submerged in nets left underwater in Braddock's Bay, Irondequoit Bay, and the lake, but the Coast Guard almost never made contact with the smugglers. In

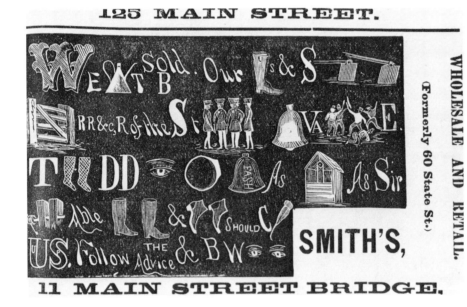

125 MAIN STREET.

WHOLESALE AND RETAIL.

(Formerly 60 State St.)

SMITH'S,

11 MAIN STREET BRIDGE.

ROCHESTER SEED STORE
AND AGRICULTURAL WAREHOUSE.
NO. 29 BUFFALO ST., OPPOSITE THE ARCADE.

Garden and Field Seeds, of our own growth, and imported from London ; also a large assortment of choice FLOWER SEEDS.
AGRICULTURAL & HORTICULTURAL
IMPLEMENTS OF ALL KINDS.
Horse Powers, Threshers and Separators, Reapers, Plows, Cultivators, Hay Cutters, Corn Shellers, Seed Planters, &c. &c. Bird Seed by the bushel, &c. &c.   JAMES P. FOGG & BROTHER.

one instance a fifty-foot Coast Guard picket was patrolling the Lake Ontario coast east of the city about 4:00 A.M. when a crewman noticed a red light among the trees on shore. As the boat moved in a lantern and men could be seen.

Suddenly the guards saw a long, low boat in the dim, early morning light. When the boat ignored a command to heave to, a machine gun was fired over the boat. The engines of the smugglers' boat started. As it made its way into the lake, it pulled up close to the Coast Guard boat and sped off with the guard in close pursuit, firing as many as 650 shots from the machine gun on its deck. Gunfire from rifles or revolvers was returned and the guards took cover. But with ammunition and fuel running low, the guard was unable to stay in pursuit and they headed back to port in Summerville.

Though there was a bootlegging business in Rochester, many people also made their own brew at home for their weddings, baptisms, and other celebrations and speakeasies flourished. The return of the breweries in 1934 provided jobs badly needed during the Great Depression, but temperance advocates were not defeated. In 1938 one spokesman promised that the return of Prohibition was "as certain as the rising sun." Though it was intended to end the curses of alcohol, the Prohibition laws instead created a revolution in lifestyles that had a lasting effect.

GEORGE EASTMAN AND OTHER INFLUENTIAL ROCHESTERIANS

In an office in the rear of the Rochester Community Savings Bank on Main Street, a young man named George Eastman worked quietly as a bank clerk. For years, Rochesterians, held motionless by a metal stand, stood before photographers to have formal portraits done. Eastman changed this. He worked with a photographer friend to develop a practical dry plate ready-made to sell to photographers. In 1880 he set up a workshop above a music store on State Street to manufacture the plates. He organized the Eastman Dry Plate Company in 1884 and four years later patented the Kodak box camera. George Eastman's Kodak camera caught on despite the depression as many people bought the twenty-five dollar camera. The one hundred-frame film that came with the camera was returned to Eastman's company and for ten dollars it was developed and printed and the camera reloaded. His slogan, "You press the button, we do the rest." attracted many buyers. A camera in the hands of so many private people not only made photography less formal, but the success of the Eastman Dry Plate and Film Company allowed Eastman to expand his State Street plant and to open a new

This clever advertisement for Smith's Shoes appeared in the Rochester City Directory in 1870. It reads, "We can't be undersold. Our boots and shoes, gators et cetera are of the highest possible (posse-bell) value (v-hallow-e). Those (th-those) desiring fashionable (fashion-a-bell) as well as servicable (sir-vice-able) boots and gators should count on us. Follow the advice and be wise." Smith's was one of the businesses built on the Main Street Bridge.
From the 1870 Rochester City Directory at the Rochester Public Library

The Rochester Seed Store in an advertisement in the Rochester City Directory for 1950. Michael Bateham took over the Rochester Seed Store in the Reynolds' Arcade in 1837. When George Ellwanger arrived in Rochester in 1835, he soon became manager of Bateham's Rochester Seed Store. City and country people both found varieties and qualities of seeds that popularized the planting of gardens in Rochester.
From the Rochester Public Library

Jesse Hatch was one of Rochester's earliest shoemakers. He began making custom shoes in his shop on Buffalo Street. He was the first shoemaker in the city to hire women to finish shoes and the first to manufacture baby shoes. His ability to modernize and mass produce helped him to survive an increasingly more competitive market as the Erie Canal brought in shoes manufactured in the east and Rochester's shoes had to appeal to the east and other markets.
From an engraving at the Rochester Public Library

Women working in the clothing industry assembling clothes at Fashion Park around 1925.
Donated to the Office of the City Historian; courtesy of Bonnie Deisenroth

Flags flew from every window of one building as the horse-drawn fire equipment passed under the arch of electric lights. This photograph is undated, but the first Industrial Exposition was held in 1908 and the fire horses were retired in 1927. People stood on the balcony of the center building and leaned out of the windows. Notice the sailor outfit on the little boy in the left foreground above the letter.
From St. John Fisher College Library

This advertisement for Hatch Shoes appeared in the 1853 Rochester City Directory. Many advertisements of this sort were from the printer's premade designs and did not always reflect a true picture of the business or activities in the store. Nevertheless it is an interesting advertisement showing women and children trying on shoes, while sitting on the floor.
From the Office of the City Historian

"Rochester Made Means Quality," was the slogan coined by the Chamber of Commerce to emphasize the quality of Rochester's products. The slogan was used with another spelling on this 1920 cover of sheet music with words written by Kendrick Shedd, a University of Rochester professor. It was used in the 1920 Rochester Industrial Exposition.
From the Rochester Public Library

plant called Kodak Park.

Eastman eventually manufactured film, the Kodak camera, and flexible motion picture film. He was struggling to develop a flexible film for his still-shot Kodak camera when Thomas Edison invented the moving picture camera. Edison's camera could take still-shots in rapid succession, but he did not have a flexible film to make it work. In 1889, Eastman perfected his film and on hearing of it, Edison sent for it immediately. The combination of Eastman's film and Edison's camera created the motion picture industry and brought the two inventors together in a life-long friendship.

Eastman himself became a strong force in the city, though he never ran for political office. He donated two hundred thousand dollars in 1900 to Mechanic's Institute to insure himself a steady supply of skilled employees. He gave sixty-seven thousand dollars to the University of Rochester to build a physics building and one hundred thousand dollars to an endowment fund. Eastman funded dental clinics and his employees benefited from a one hundred thousand dollar fund towards their education as well as an annual wage dividend. He founded the Center for Governmental Research in 1915. He donated four hundred thousand dollars towards the reconstruction of the City's General Hospital in 1909. He built the Eastman Theatre for the "enrichment of Community Life" and funded the Rochester Philharmonic Orchestra.

Edison's death on October 18, 1931, brought sorrow to Eastman who was concerned that he would be a burden in his own declining years. He ended his own life on March 14, 1932. His ashes were buried under a monument at Kodak Park on Lake Avenue.

There were other photographic developments in the city. While working in the patent department of a New York electronics company, Chester Carlson began to work on his idea of the duplication of documents and drawings that he called "electrophotography." In 1938 he successfully made the first dry ink, electrostatic copy. He patented the "electrophotographic copier system in 1940 and after a demonstration at Batelle Memorial Institute in Columbus, Ohio, he interested Batelle Development Corporation in further development. The Haloid Company, which had been involved in the manufacture of photocopy and photographic paper since 1908, began commercial development of Carlson's copier in 1945. Naming the copier system Xerox, meaning in Greek "dry write," Haloid improved the copier with the introduction of each new model and it became increas-

ingly more popular.

Just before Eastman developed the camera, George B. Selden designed the first gasoline-powered automobile. He filed a patent application in 1879, but repeatedly amended the application. After he lost a lengthy battle over patent rights with Henry Ford, Selden and his sons assembled automobiles for other manufacturers and from 1907 to 1916, Selden maufactured luxury automobiles. In 1913 he began to produce trucks until 1930 when Bethlehem Truck company of Pennsylvania bought the company.

James Cunningham's Carriage Factory began in 1838 to build carriages of all types, specializing in hearses, funeral carriages, and ambulances. Transportation through the early decades of the century was continuously changing and demanded that a company change with it in order to survive. Cunningham survived more than a century by diversification and adaptation to the changing lifestyles. In 1908 it began to manufacture luxury gasoline-driven automobiles. In 1928 Cunningham formed Cunningham-Hall Aircraft Corporation and manufactured airplanes as well as automobiles. During the world wars it produced military equipment, tanks and armored vehicles. After the Second World War it began to manufacture electronic components for the broadcasting industry. One hundred and thirty years after it began to produce carriages, and still a strong company, Cunningham was bought by Gleason Works.

The automobile had begun to change transportation as well as industrial enterprise. Not only Selden and Cunningham were involved in the development of gasoline-driven transportation. In 1908 Edward A. and Joseph C. Halbleib began to manufacture coils and repair electric motors for the company they organized, Rochester Coil Company. In 1926 General Motors purchased Rochester Coil Company and the North East Electric Company, founded in 1909 by James J. Stafford for the production of electric starting and lighting systems. The combined companies prospered during the Depression and in 1938 separated to become Delco Appliance (later Delco Products) and Rochester Products, both General Motors Divisions.

Architectural designs were changing lifestyles as well. Skyscrapers were being built around the country. Architect James Cutler designed a mail chute to streamline mail collection in the skyscrapers. When it won the approval of the U.S. Post Office, Cutler's mail chutes became popular and Cutler became wealthy.

H. H. Warner became wealthy fulfilling another need—patent medicine. Medicines were not tightly regulated and many, like Warner's, were high

An advertisement for the Rochester Brewing Company from the 1874 Rochester City Directory.

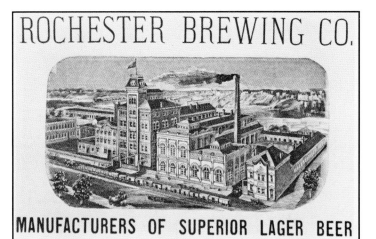

ROCHESTER BREWING CO.

MANUFACTURERS OF SUPERIOR LAGER BEER

The W. B. Duffy Cider Company; from the 1880 Rochester City Directory.

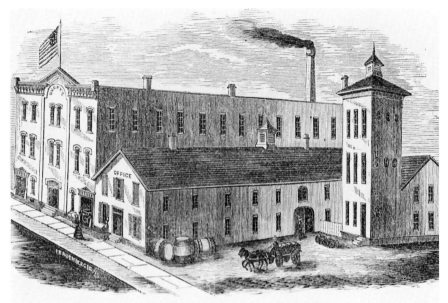

W. B. DUFFY CIDER CO.,

Rochester celebrated the Centennial of the settlement of Rochester in 1911 with the opening of Exposition Park (later Edgerton Park) on the site of the old Western House of Refuge, now the State Industrial School at Industry, New York.
From St. John Fisher College Library

Bartholomay Brewery from the 1874 Rochester City Directory. When Prohibition became effective in 1920, Bartholomay became a dairy.

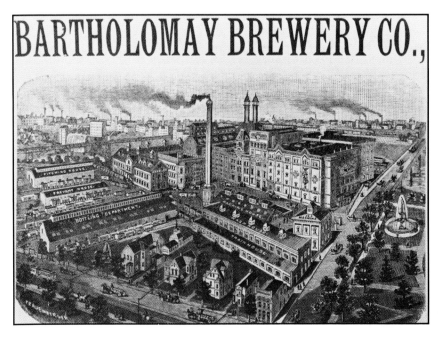

BARTHOLOMAY BREWERY CO.,

When Prohibition was repealed in 1934, the Genesee Brewing Company wagon was pulled through the streets by two ornately decorated draft horses to advertise, "Coming soon! Genesee Liebotschoner. The beer you didn't forget."
From Gannett Newspaper

Advertisement for the Miller Brewing Company in The City of Rochester, Illustrated.
Published by the Post Express Printing Company, 1890

George Eastman, second from left, and
Thomas Edison, center, together at
Eastman's home on East Avenue in 1928.
Eastman's Kodacolor motion pictures were
first demonstrated on July 25, 1928, at
Eastman's home. The other men are not
identified.
From the Rochester Public Library

Eastman was visited by many well known
and distinguished people like Comdr.
Richard E. Byrd, South Pole explorer, in
the 1920s.
From the Rochester Public Library

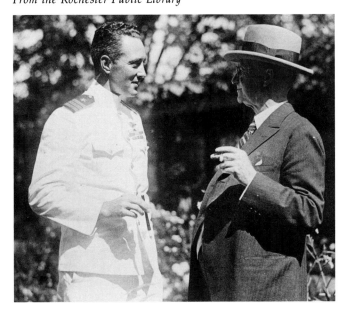

in alcoholic content. He made a fortune selling his Warner's Safe Liver Cure and he was creative in marketing. He sold his product in colorfully illustrated packages. In 1881, he attached his name to the famed astronomer Lewis Swift by building him an observatory. The public helped to raise the money for the telescope and it was open to the public by paying either twenty-five cents or a wrapper from Warner's Safe Liver Cure. Warner lost his fortune during the panic of 1893.

Rochester became internationally known for its production of lenses. In 1852, John Jacob Bausch and Henry Lomb began producing eyeglasses and other optical products, selling them from their store in Reynolds' Arcade. Bausch's development of hard rubber frames for eyeglasses helped to make the company successful. They were soon filling orders for Europe.

Bausch and Lomb began producing photographic lenses, microscopes, binoculars, and telescopes. During World War I the company increased production of binoculars, telescopes, rangefinders, and searchlights, employing six thousand people. During World War II, the company won recognition for maximum war production. Over more than a century, Bausch and Lomb has expanded its production to include contact lenses and eye examination computers.

Many other companies helped to make Rochester's industrial base strong: Gleason works which manufactures gears; Rochester Button Company; Stromberg-Carlson which produced telephone equipment and later television and radio equipment; and Sybron Corporation, an amalgamation of Ritter Dental Equipment Company, Pfaudler, Taylor Instruments, Wilmot-Castle, and Nagle. Sybron now manufactures health products, instruments, and chemicals.

Professor Henry A. Ward and Lewis Henry Morgan influenced the lives of Rochesterians too, though not by manufacturing. Professor Henry A. Ward organized Ward's Natural Science Establishment. He traveled world-wide collecting specimens of plants, animals, and minerals for sale to laboratories and museums. Lewis Henry Morgan was an attorney but his study of the Iroquois culture earned him the title of "father of American Anthropolgy."

George Eastman on a big game hunt in Africa in July, 1928. Dr. Albert Kaiser, Rochester's Health Officer, stands on the right. Eastman poses with his rifle near British hunter Philip Percival. Osa Johnson stands next to Eastman.
From the Rochester Public Library

George Eastman in the front at the far left as a young bank clerk at the Rochester Savings Bank in the 1880s.
From the Rochester Public Library

1891

George Eastman photographed with one of his own cameras on board a ship at the turn of the century. After the development of this camera, many people could photograph their vacations.
From the Rochester Public Library

The Eastman Kodak Company factory in 1891. The slogan "You Press the Button, We Do The Rest," sold thousands of cameras.
Postcard from the Rochester Public Library

When George Eastman developed the Kodak camera, photography moved out of the professional studio into the lives of everyday people. The subjects changed from formally posed photographs to critical moments in a baseball game or Johnny's first step. The early Kodaks were loaded with one hundred shots. When the roll was taken, the entire camera was returned to Kodak for developing, printing, and reloading.
Postcard from St. John Fisher College Library

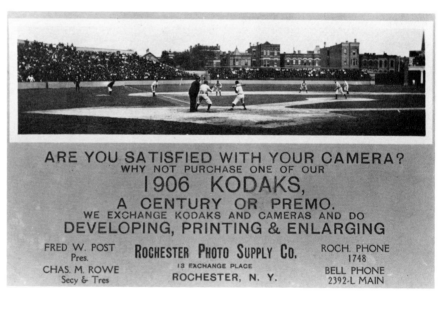

ARE YOU SATISFIED WITH YOUR CAMERA?
WHY NOT PURCHASE ONE OF OUR
1906 KODAKS,
A CENTURY OR PREMO.
WE EXCHANGE KODAKS AND CAMERAS AND DO
DEVELOPING, PRINTING & ENLARGING

FRED W. POST
Pres.
CHAS. M. ROWE
Secy & Tres

ROCHESTER PHOTO SUPPLY CO.
13 EXCHANGE PLACE
ROCHESTER, N. Y.

ROCH. PHONE
1748
BELL PHONE
2392-L MAIN

The Eastman Theatre opened in 1922. It was given to the University of Rochester by George Eastman "For the Enrichment of Community Life." The university received millions of dollars from Eastman who also funded the Rochester Philharmonic, the School of Medicine and Dentistry and several dental dispensaries around the nation and the world.
From the Rochester Public Library

George Selden successfully tested his design for a gasoline driven automobile in 1877 in New York, but he lost a patent battle with Henry Ford in 1911. This photograph was taken in the 1930s at an unidentified location.
From the Rochester Public Library

George B. Selden (1846-1922) filed a patent application in 1879 for the first "road engine" powered by the internal combustion engine. Though recognized as the inventor of the gasoline-driven automobile, Henry Ford challenged Selden's claim to a patent and won after a lengthy legal battle. Selden and his sons assembled automobiles for other manufacturers after 1905 and began to produce their own cars and trucks in Rochester from 1907 to 1916. In 1913 Selden Truck Sales Corporation produced trucks until 1930 when Bethlehem Truck Company of Pennsylvania bought it.
From the Charles Zoller Collection at the International Museum of Photography at George Eastman House

The James Cunningham Carriage Factory opened in 1838 and grew to be one of the largest carriage manufacturers in the world. Cunningham made carriages of all types, but specialized in hearses, funeral carriages, and ambulances. By 1908, Cunningham was producing luxury gasoline-driven automobiles. In 1928 Cunningham branched out into Cunningham-Hall Aircraft Corporation manufacturing the airplane in which George Eastman took his first airplane ride. Cunningham produced luxury automobiles until 1937, military equipment, tanks, and armored vehicles during World War I and World War II and by the 1950s produced electronic components for the broadcasting industry. It survived for over one hundred years by adaptation and diversification. In 1968, Cunningham became a division of Gleason Works.
Advertisement from the 1849-1850 Rochester City Directory

James B. Cutler (1848-1927) invented the Cutler mail chute in 1879 and installed the first one in America in the Elwood Building in Rochester at the corner of Main and State streets. That building was torn down in the 1960s, but the Gannett Newspapers Building on the corner of Exchange and Broad streets still has the Cutler mail chute. The mail chute won the approval of the U.S. Post Office and was installed in the new skyscrapers being built in the late 1800s. Cutler became wealthy on the invention. He was also an architect and businessman. He was Rochester's mayor from 1904 to 1908.
From the Rochester Public Library

H. H. Warner (1842-1923) made a fortune selling the Warner's Safe Liver Cure in colorfully illustrated packages. The "patent medicine king" served as the first president of the Rochester Chamber of Commerce and built a magnificent cast iron building on St. Paul Street that bore his initial in medallions on the front. He built a castle-like mansion on East Avenue and financed the one hundred thousand dollar Warner Observatory for Professor Lewis Swift. He lost his fortune during the panic of 1893 after he doubled his company's capital stock, sold the company to British businessmen, then lost his profits in a copper mine.
From an engraving by Atlantic Publishing and Engraving Company, at the Rochester Public Library

Prof. Lewis Swift (1820-1913) inside the Warner Observatory. The twenty-foot telescope with a sixteen inch lens magnified objects two thousand times. Rochester's cloudy ceiling did not afford the opportunity for astronomers that the California sky offered, but Swift did discover four new comets.
From the Rochester Public Library

The Warner Observatory was built on East Avenue by patent medicine king H. H. Warner for Lewis Swift, a Rochester hardware dealer whose avocation for astronomy won his four international medals for the discovery of comets. The observatory opened in 1882 with a twenty-two foot telescope and a sixteen inch objective lens that magnified objects two thousand times. The top of the dome of the observatory was sixty-five feet above the ground with a diameter of thirty-one feet. Public subscription paid for the telescope as well as one of the sidereal clocks. The other was donated by Alonzo Watson of the University of Michigan. A spectroscope was donated by Hiram Sibley, organizer of Western Union Telegraph Company. The public was admitted at times by presenting the wrapper of H. H. Warner's Safe Liver Cure or by buying a twenty-five cent ticket. When Warner's business failed in the panic of 1893, Swift moved his telescope to Pasadena, California.
From the Rochester Public Library

In the late 1870s Prof. Lewis Swift could be found lying on a rug on the roof of the Duffy's Cider Mill on White Street where he could have an unobstructed view of the stars. Sometimes, he spent the entire night lying on the rug under the telescope. Sometimes, a newspaper reporter or a curious citizen climbed the three ladders leading to the roof to learn what the professor was seeing. Several times, Professor Swift excited the community when he discovered a new comet. Swift scurried down the ladders and caught a horse-drawn streetcar to the city where he sent off a telegram to the Dudley Observatory in Albany or later in the decade to the observatory in Vienna. Swift waited tensely for confirmation of his discoveries and five times was honored by the naming of "Swift" comets in 1877, 1878, 1879, 1880, and 1881. Swift viewed the stars from the roof of the Powers' Building, dark alleys, and even his own backyard on Ambrose Street. The gas lights on the streets and the glare of flickering gas and oil lamps in private homes disturbed his work, but he finally found an unobstructed view on the roof of Duffy's Cider Mill. Swift was later rewarded with the construction of the Warner Observatory and an interested public responded with generous donations to purchase the telescope.
From the Office of the City Historian from a broadside done after a photograph taken on July 4, 1880; appeared in the Union & Advertiser August 13, 1892

Grinding lenses at Bausch and Lomb about 1938.
From the Rochester Public Library

Prof. Henry A. Ward (1834-1906) in a contemplative mood in his study. Ward was a naturalist who traveled worldwide to collect specimens for his Natural Science Establishment. He sold plant, animal, and mineral collections to laboratories and museums. He stuffed several animals for P. T. Barnum, including the twelve-foot elephant "Jumbo" who appeared in Rochester in 1881. His museum was located on College Avenue opposite the University of Rochester's early campus on Prince Street. Ward was a grandson of pioneer Levi Ward.
From the Rochester Public Library

An early advertisement for J. J. Bausch's Optical Company before he joined with Henry Lomb in 1853 to form Bausch and Lomb Optical Company.
From the Rochester Public Library

Ernst Gundlach made the first microscopes produced in Rochester in 1875 for Bausch and Lomb Company. He later founded the Gundlach Optical Company.
From the Rochester Public Library

Lewis Henry Morgan (1818-1881) was an attorney whose study and writings on the Iroquois culture made a lasting contribution to education and earned him the title of the "father of American anthropology."
From the Rochester Public Library

The second Monroe County Court House from an engraving in W. H. McIntosh's History of Monroe County, *From the Office of the City Historian*

Main Street from W. H. McIntosh's History of Monroe County, *1877*

Straub's Commercial Block on Lake Avenue in 1877. From an engraving in W. H. McIntosh's History of Monroe County; *the Office of the City Historian*

From W. H. McIntosh's History of Monroe County, *1877*

Stagecoaches and horsecars carried passengers to and from the Clinton Hotel on Exchange Street in the 1870s. From W. H. McIntosh's History of Monroe County, *1877*

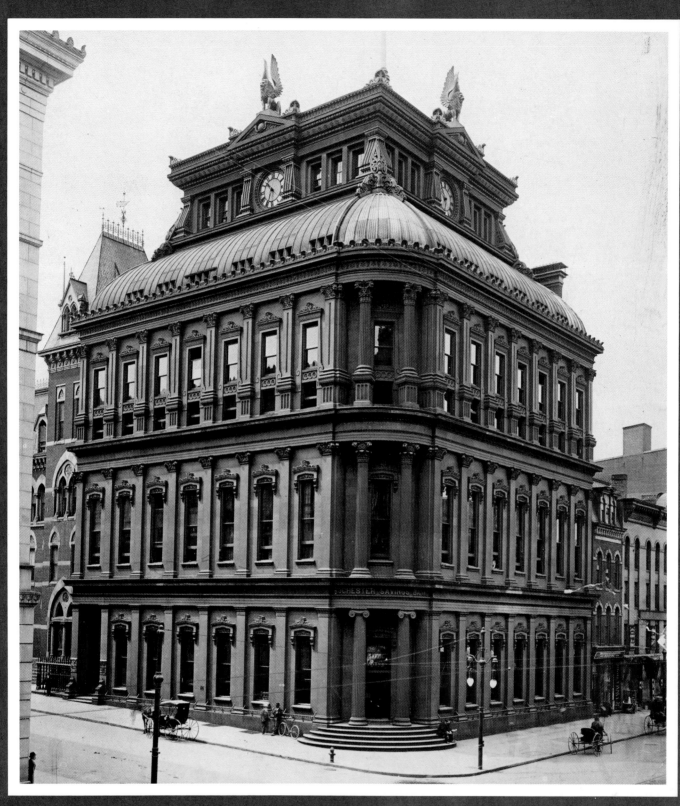

The Rochester Savings Bank at the corner of Main Street and Fitzhugh in the 1890s. This building was one of the most delightful architectural buildings in the city. George Eastman worked as a bank clerk in the rear of this building while he worked in the evenings at a rented State Street office making dry plates for commercial photographers. Look at the ornate embellishments on the top of the building and the columns on every floor. Double gaslights hang light arms from the light pole in front of the building. Notice two men in caps sitting on the steps of the bank reviewing papers. Four carriages, one very ornate in the lower left corner, await their drivers at the edge of the street. The Monroe County Office Building is visible on the left.
From the Rochester Public Library

Meta Baker (Mrs. Theodore Steinhausen) posed for this photograph in 1892 in recognition of the four hundredth anniversary of Columbus' discovery of America.
From the Rochester Public Library

A policeman stands on the corner near the Monroe County Court House in the 1890s. The corner of the Cogwell Fountain is visible on the right.
From the Rochester Public Library

The Rochester Herald displayed the newspaper in the window of their office where a crowd of men and young boys gathered to read as soon as it was printed. The postcard from which the photograph was taken is not dated.
Postcard from St. John Fisher College

Repairs being done to the Statue of Justice on the second Monroe County Court House cupola. Note the captain's chair straddling the roof at the base of the cupola. St. Luke's Church is on the left. The second courthouse was built in the early 1850s.
From the Rochester Public Library

The old Court Street Bridge was destroyed in the flood of 1887. Telephone poles are prevented from being carried away only by the wires that hold them to the bridge. Debris is carried downriver as three men stand dangerously close to the falling decking of the old bridge.
From the Rochester Public Library

A resident of the Jewish Home for the Aged blew the ram's horn to signal the beginning of the new Jewish year in September of 1937. Eastern European Jews were among the many immigrants that chose to make Rochester their home in the early decades of this century.
From the Rochester Public Library

The cornerstone of the Hebrew Charities building was laid on May 4, 1913. This photograph captured the hundreds of people who attended to see the opening of what became the Baden Street Settlement House. The Settlement House was organized in 1901 to meet the needs of poor Eastern European Jews who settled the northeastern part of Rochester where housing was older and more affordable. Since then the Settlement House has continually met the changing needs of the various immigrant groups that have settled in the neighborhood. Several religious organizations and the Lewis Street Settlement House, the Montgomery Neighborhood Center, and the Charles House meet the needs of Italians, blacks, and other newcomers respectively.
From the Rochester Public Library

Many immigrants found ready jobs in heavy labor needed to lay new sewers, water pipes, streetcar, and railroad tracks. Men in the early decades of the century are laying pipe here for the city. From the City Photo Laboratory

Holy Redeemer Church at the corner of Hudson and Clifford Avenues was for decades the gathering place of hundreds of European newcomers. Its twin steeples are landmarks visible at a great distance. From the Office of the City Historian

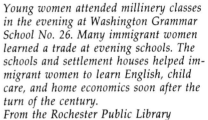

Young women attended millinery classes in the evening at Washington Grammar School No. 26. Many immigrant women learned a trade at evening schools. The schools and settlement houses helped immigrant women to learn English, child care, and home economics soon after the turn of the century.
From the Rochester Public Library

A. Millman and Sons at the corner of Main and North streets. Millman is chatting with a friend as another friend ambles down North Street.
From St. John Fisher College

Waiting for customers outside of Schmidt and Kaelber Opticians at the turn of the century.
From the Rochester Public Library

Chapter Six

Men wait at their wagons on Main Street in this pre-1932 photograph by Charles Zoller. Notice the bushel baskets and burlap bags of food across the street at Deavenport's. In the far left is the Musee Theatre. The streetlights are protected by mesh over the globes.
From the International Museum of Photography at George Eastman House

AFTER THE WAR:
The Civic Growth Of Rochester

IMPROVING THE HEALTH OF THE CITY

In the late nineteenth century Rochester continued to be plagued by epidemics: diptheria, smallpox, tuberculosis, typhoid, childhood diseases, and miscellaneous infant bowel disorders commonly called "summer complaint."

Many of the diseases were spread more rapidly by the mobile population that traveled by canal, rail, streetcar, and stagecoach. Quarantine orders helped to check the spread of diseases, but eliminating the source was the only way to prevent them. In the 1870s drinking water was brought from Hemlock Lake and the city was assured of having enough water even in summer to keep the sewers flushed. Indoor toilets were becoming more common, though outhouses were not unusual.

Wells for drinking water were replaced by taps in the kitchen and indoor bathtubs had running water. Ice delivered to homes was sometimes cut from contaminated ponds and continued to be a health problem.

Children under five were most often the victims of disease and hundreds of them died every year. In the 1890s Health Officer George Goler began a clean milk campaign. He believed that children were dying from tainted milk that caused a bacterial diarrhea that so dehydrated the child that it died. Children under one year whose diets were solely milk were especially vulnerable. Milkmen rolled their wagons through the neighborhood streets ladling milk into household jars from milk cans sitting out in the hot sun. Without proper refrigeration, the milk spoiled. Goler set up nurses'

stations to sell fresh pasteurized milk in sterile bottles. He tested cows for tuberculosis and licensed milkmen. He educated mothers on childcare and immigrant women were given additional training in childcare and housekeeping by settlement houses.

Giving birth was also the cause of many deaths. Midwives practiced with little or no training and many doctors signed birth certificates for them. Many midwives could not read or speak English and so could not follow medicinal labels. The deaths of many new mothers from "childbed fever," was caused by unclean instruments and unwashed hands. Goler fought to license midwives and to require doctors to file birth and death certificates.

Most births were in the home. Hospitals were for the sick. The first hospital, the City Hospital, was incorporated by the Rochester Female Charitable Society in 1847; but without a building, a site, or money it was unable to serve the community. In 1857, the Sisters of Charity organized St. Mary's Hospital in two wooden stables. Among their early patients were three thousand Civil War soldiers. Soon the hospital moved out of the stables into a four-story stone building built on the grounds. In 1864 St. Mary's began running an ambulance service. Fresh vegetables were brought in from their Chili farm.

Finally in 1857, a site was chosen on the old cemetery on Buffalo Road for a four-story brick building to house the City Hospital which opened in 1864. City Hospital grew, adding wings in 1865 and 1871. In 1911, City Hospital became Rochester General Hospital. The Northside opened in 1956 and the Westside was closed ten years later.

Hahneman Hospital opened in 1889 and later became Highland Hospital. In 1887 the Rochester Homeopathic Hospital opened and became Genesee Hospital in 1926.

The Municipal Hospital, originally a pesthouse for the control of infectious diseases, became affiliated with the University of Rochester's teaching hospital, Strong Memorial Hospital. In 1963 the hospital was sold to the university.

After 1826 the poor were cared for at the Monroe County Poorhouse on South Avenue. In 1967, the hospital was renamed Monroe Community Hospital. Park Avenue Hospital became Park Ridge Hospital. Several other private hospitals also opened, but closed as other hospitals grew.

TRAVELING IN LATE NINETEENTH-CENTURY ROCHESTER

Newspaper editor Thurlow Weed complained in mid-century that young Rochesterians had no idea what travel was like in his lifetime. Early pioneers walked, rode horseback, or pushed their ox carts and wagons along trails barely wide enough to accommodate them and sometimes so poorly marked that they became lost. Travel was both uncomfortable and dangerous, for there were wild animals and accidents. Sometimes the water at the fords was too high or the current was too swift and many a pioneer had a chilling story of near death. The main streets of the early settlements were impassable with a wagon because of tree stumps that had not yet rotted away or been pulled. Later stagecoach travelers sometimes had to get out of the coach to lighten it and sometimes even lifted the coach from muddy ditches.

But travel improved as the roads and bridges were built. Lake schooners that traveled along the shore and to Canada became more numerous and the port was improved. Stagecoaches went to more towns and the railroad competed with the Erie Canal that by the end of the century was diminishing in its importance. Boatyards began to disappear. Horse-drawn streetcars shared the streets with bicycles by the 1890s. By the early 1900s, the electric trolley replaced the horse-drawn trolley and automobiles were seen on the streets.

The hay market was gradually replaced by the gasoline station and stables and barns became garages and parking lots. The automobile demanded the improvement of roads and extended the distance one could travel in a day. In the first few decades of the century, Rochesterians built airplanes and flew them even before the airport was built in 1918. The change in transportation changed our lifestyle, perhaps never so rapidly as at the turn of the century.

THE THEATRE IN ROCHESTER

By the end of the Civil War the theatre was an accepted form of entertainment. Many famous actors and actresses appeared in the city including Edwin Booth and Sarah Bernhardt. Vaudeville, minstrels, and traveling shows entertained throughout the century, even after the introduction of Edison's new invention—the moving picture.

Moving pictures first were shown in Rochester on January 18, 1895, through the Kinetoscope, a little box with a peep hole through which the viewer could see moving dancers or boxers for only a nickel. The Kinetoscope used Eastman's celluloid film. In the summer of 1896, moving pictures were projected on a screen at the Lyceum Theatre by an Edison Kinematograph. A short comedy about a fisherman being knocked from his boat by a wagon passing over a bridge was shown at the Central Presbyterian Church that same year.

The Bijou Dream was built in 1906 at East Main and North Water streets as the only theatre devoted to moving pictures. Its lights gave the theatre a Broadway atmosphere. Movie houses quickly became popular.

But sound movies were not well received. James Moore first brought the movie to the Temple Theatre on South Clinton Avenue as a vaudeville act in 1913 after seeing Edison's Kinetophone, a synchronized record and movie, at Menlo Park. The audience was apathetic as others around the country were and apprehensive movie producers continued to make half of their movies silent. Sound movies were not shown again in the city until 1927 when Fay's Theatre on West Main Street again tested the audience. The following year, Eastman Theatre and many others began to show sound movies to interested audiences. What saved the sound movies may have been the introduction of favored silent screen and Broadway stage actors to Hollywood. Whatever the reason, Rochester's theatres were changed.

Refuse disposal in open horse-drawn wagons often caused contamination of the streets and the spread of disease. Early outhouses were emptied by scavengers licensed by the city to haul away the contents. Often they were dumped into the river from the bridges at night, thus the term "night soil." New sewers helped to carry away water that at one time caused typhoid and other diseases when it bred mosquitoes or stagnated. Water from Hemlock Lake piped to the city in the 1870s helped to eliminate the stagnated sewers and resulting toxic gases, but much work remained to be done in improving refuse disposal. Today space and the safe disposal of refuse remain problems.
From the City Bureau of Public Information

Washing the city's streets helped to prevent disease. In the late 1920s, a Department of Public Works truck washes a neighborhood street.
From the Rochester Public Library

THE ESTABLISHMENT OF THE CITY PARKS

The pioneers had no need for parks. They were surrounded by the natural beauty of the wilderness. Many pioneers recalled their visits to the Upper Falls to watch the spray as the water dashed against the rocks ninety-six feet below. In the winter the mist formed ice crystals on the rock face of the falls.

But the rapidly increasing population required more recreational space. It outgrew the town squares set aside by the early developers for courthouses that were never built. Children played in the streets, flew kites in empty fields, and swam in the river and canal. Baseball became popular after the Civil War, but there were no ball fields. Circuses set up in the decreasing number of empty lots and on the outskirts of town. Many people traveled to resorts on the lake front.

In 1888, the city accepted the gift of twenty acres from Ellwanger and Barry Nursery which became Highland Park, the nucleus of today's Rochester Parks System. New parks were established and Mount Hope Cemetery, the city's first municipally-owned cemetery, came under the control of the Parks Department.

After much controversy over the design of the parks, Frederick Law Olmsted's plan to emphasize the beauty of the Genesee with a north and south park was adopted and Maplewood, Seneca, and Genesee Valley Parks were created. Children found safe swimming, boating, hiking, skiing, and camping sites in the parks and no longer had to play in the streets. With the shorter working day, families found more leisure time for the parks. Many of the species of plants and trees originally a part of the nursery, still grow at Highland Park, the city's first park, established a century ago.

FIREFIGHTING IN THE LATE NINETEENTH CENTURY

Firefighting seemed to move into a modern age in 1874 when the Holly System brought high pressure water into the city to enable firefighters to reach the upper floors of the multi-story buildings being built. Fire was the greatest hazard faced by the city, for unlike floods, it was unpredictable and more frequent.

In the early days when fire broke out, church bells and fire bells rang out the code for the district and volunteer firemen raced to the fire pushing hose carts. In winter the water in the races or the canal was sometimes frozen and in the summer it was often inadequate.

Citizens were required to keep fire buckets ready and to join with firefighters in extinguishing the blaze. In 1829 the bucket brigade gave way to the fire engine and ladder apparatus. After 1832, Rochester had six fire engines and a ladder apparatus.

There were numerous fires. Among the most disastrous was the Main Street Bridge fire in 1834, the burning of the flour mills in Brown's Race in 1887 and the Sibley, Lindsey and Curr fire in 1904. The Brown's Race fire occurred in December of 1887 when naptha was accidentally sent through sewer pipes from the Vacuum Oil Works to the Municipal Gas Company. A spark, possibly from one of the mills, set off a series of explosions. Eyewitnesses hearing the blasts, watched the progress of the fire as manhole covers blew several hundred feet from one intersection after another. Several buildings caught fire including the Jefferson, Washington, and Clinton Mills. Five men lost their lives.

The fire horses were replaced by gasoline engines in 1927 after a deadly hoof disease disabled most of the horses. The old horse-drawn pumpers were a favorite in parades.

St. Mary's Hospital was first opened in a barn by the Sisters of Charity in 1857. They treated wounded soldiers during the Civil War.
From the Rochester Public Library

Dr. Sarah Adamson Dolley was a graduate of Central Medical College, Eclectic, in Rochester and was one of the first female medical students in the country. From the Edward G. Miner Library, University of Rochester

Dr. George Goler (1864-1940) was the official City Health Officer when he headed the local movement to professionalize medicine. He opposed worthless patent medicines and dangerous nonprescription drugs like Kopp's Baby's Friend, a codeine syrup intended to quiet sick babies, but sometimes given in overdose. Goler struggled to require birth and death certificates and to license midwives, many of whom were immigrants who could not speak English or read medicine labels. Many new mothers died of childbed fever caused by contamination introduced inside of the mother by unclean hands or instruments.
From the Rochester Public Library

Hope Hospital as it appeared in 1902. Its
large white canvas tents offered temporary shelter for the ill.
From the Rochester Public Library

Inside the crude shelter of Hope Hospital,
three young patients warm themselves by
the stove.
From the Rochester Public Library

This contagious hospital on River Road near Clarissa Street was more commonly known as the Pest House where people with contagious diseases were quarantined. After the smallpox epidemic of 1901, the hospital was torn down. Smallpox epidemics spread through Rochester in 1901 and 1904. Cholera epidemics spread in 1832, 1834, 1849, and 1852. In the nineteenth century, newspapers tracked the deadly smallpox and typhoid as they spread nearer to Rochester. The migration of the population by canal, lake, and railroad made the spread of contagious diseases more rapid and more difficult to control. In 1904, Dr. George Goler, the city health officer, started the Municipal Hospital for contagious diseases and treatment of the poor as well. That hospital became Strong Memorial Hospital.
From the Rochester Public Library

The Monroe County Almshouse was part of a complex of county buildings that included a hospital that became Monroe Community Hospital in 1967.
From the Rochester Public Library

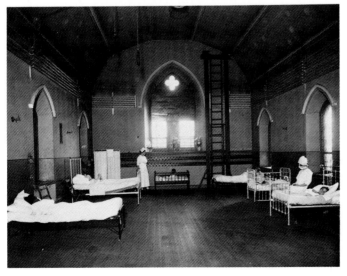

The influenza epidemic of 1918 sickened so many people, the hospitals could not contain them all. A temporary hospital was set up at the Gannett House.
From the Rochester Public Library

93

The Municipal Hospital in 1908. Sheep grazing in the fields nearby were sometimes used in experiments.
From the Rochester Public Library

The older Rochester General Hospital was incorporated in 1847 and first opened its doors in 1864. The old building was torn down and the new building was named the Northside Hospital.
From the Rochester Public Library

Hospital bazaars were common ways for ladies and societies to raise money. In 1863, Mrs. Montgomery, Levi Ward, and Mrs. Theodore A. Ives raised money for an unidentified hospital.
From the Rochester Public Library

Belvidere Hospital at 593 Mount Hope Avenue. From the Rochester Public Library

The Rochester City Hospital ambulance before ambulances were motorized. It did not contain the lifesaving equipment carried today, but simply transported the patient to the hospital. Many people were still treated at home in the early twentieth century.
From the Rochester Public Library

The Hahnemann Hospital on Rockingham Street opened in the former home of Judge Henry Selden in 1889. It became Highland Hospital and still operates today. From the Rochester Public Library

Dr. John Lee opened his hospital in 1897. From the Rochester Public Library

The beautiful landscape of Highland Park was captured on canvas by this unidentified painter.

Rochester at the Turn of the Century

Charles C. Zoller (1852-1932) is credited with being among the first to bring color photography to America. While on a trip to London in 1907, Zoller learned of a color photography process called the Autochrome. He brought a large number of the color plates to Rochester for sale and for his own use.

The Autochromes presented an impressionistic image created by its large dots of color. Though many photographers found the Autochrome inferior because of its lack of clarity, Zoller was enthusiastic about its color. He photographed gardens and homes, parks and events. He photographed special occasions at the home of George Eastman and other notable citizens. However, many of his photographs record everyday life in Rochester, making them a valuable record of life in our city at the turn of the century. Every detail of an event that occurred nearly one hundred years ago is transmitted to our eye as only a photograph can.

Zoller died in 1932 leaving more than five thousand Autochromes and several thousand black and white negatives; a fine record of our growing community. They are housed at the International Museum of Photography at George Eastman House.

Today our city is the photographic capital of the world because of the work of George Eastman, Zoller and other photographic pioneers. The images on pages 97 through 104 are from The Zoller Collection.

Unidentified children gathered for a photograph at a neighborhood park on an unknown patriotic occasion.

Admiring the beauty of Rhododendron Valley at Highland Park.

A lone man strolls along a trail at Genesee Valley Park.

Spray rises from the powerful Upper Falls. This falls can be viewed from Pont De Rennes Bridge or Upper Falls Park.

Swan boats, once a popular ride on Trout Lake at Seneca Park were featured as a parade float in the early 1900s.

This James Vick Company float from the turn of the century celebrated the flower industry that made Rochester the "Flower City."

Helen Keller was photographed in the home of Mrs. Edmond Lyons.

The first factory opened by Bausch and Lomb in 1853 is celebrated in this float in the early 1900s.

A Seneca Indian at the annual Indian Festival at Maplewood Park.

Deep snow towering over this streetcar sometimes slowed travel for days.

The Iola Sanatarium, a tuberculosis hospital, was part of the Monroe County Hospital. It is used today by the county for various government offices.
From the Rochester Public Library

Children recovering from tuberculosis rest on the lawn one morning at the Edward Mott Moore Open Air School. Moore favored fresh air to maintain health and served on the Rochester Parks Commission where he helped to increase the number of public recreational areas.
From the Rochester Public Library

The Genesee Hospital opened in 1926 on Alexander Street. It was formerly the Homeopathic Hospital.
From the Rochester Public Library

The Park Avenue Hospital was established by Dr. John F. W. Whitbeck as a private hospital. It became public in 1921 and had one hundred beds after an addition was added.
From the Rochester Public Library

Strong Memorial Hospital is affiliated with the University of Rochester School o Medicine.
From the Rochester Public Library

Every summer hundreds of vacationers and weekend excursionists traveled the New York Central line from Rochester to the steamboat dock at Charlotte. Workdays were growing shorter giving more leisure time to spend on family outings by the time this photograph was taken in 1914.
From the Rochester Public Library

These boys from School No. 26 on Washington Avenue had their own transportation decades before school buses became common. The streets were dirt, the sidewalks were wooden planks, and the buildings shown were unpainted.
From the Rochester Public Library, undated

This railroad lantern, built in 1877 by the Kelly Lamp Works, used to be a common sight on the trains in Rochester. The lantern is four feet high, with a lens twenty-four inches in diameter. William Gordon points out the company name, but the portrait on the side is not identified. It was common to carry the portrait of the person honored by their name on the engine.
From the Rochester Public Library

Rochester Railroad stations.
Postcards from St. John Fisher College
Library

Lehigh Valley R. R. Passenger Station, Rochester, N.Y.

161 Erie R. R. Depot, Rochester, N.Y.

New York Central Station, Rochester, N.Y.

Main Waiting Room,
Depot of the
New York Central Lines,
Rochester, N.Y.

Boat building was a large industry in Rochester and several towns along the Erie Canal. Several men in this undated photograph stop work on the Adelbert Whalen to pose for the camera. Notice the postman at the right of center in the foreground.
From the Rochester Public Library

Many Italians and other immigrants found employment building the Barge Canal. The site and exact location of this photograph have been lost.
From St. John Fisher College Library

The second aqueduct carried canal boats across the Genesee River until the end of the season in 1919. The Johnson and Seymour raceway runs in the foreground on the opposite side of the horses. Children played along the canal and sometimes drowned in the canal and races. The Kimball Tobacco Company sits across the river on the site of the War Memorial. Notice Mercury on top of the Kimball Tobacco Company smokestack.
From the Rochester Public Library

The hay market business at the Public Market on Front Street dwindled as automobiles replaced horses. Within a few decades gasoline stations were common at busy intersections.
From the Rochester Public Library

The Four Corners as busy at the turn of the century as it is today, shows the transition of transportation in a single view: streetcars, automobiles, bicycles, pedestrians, and a truck at the right almost opposite a wagon also used for hauling.
From the Rochester Public Library

Looking down Exchange Street at the intersection of Main, several men lay track for the streetcars.
From the Rochester Public Library

The first railroad engine arrived in Rochester by canal in 1837 for the Tonawanda Railroad. This engine was the first used on the Auburn and Rochester Railroad in 1840.
From the Rochester Public Library; donated by Richard Palmer

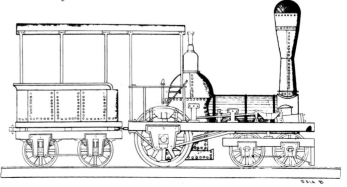

FIRST ENGINE USED ON THE AUBURN & ROCHESTER RAILROAD, 1840
Drawing presented to The Rochester Historical Society by the New York Central Railroad

Dr. William Greene opened his "airplane factory" on Belmont Street in Rochester in 1910. He scoffed at Cooley's lighter-than-air machine as early as 1895. When Cooley visited the city that year, he remarked, "My airship — I avoid the term 'flying machine,' for you know that the person Green rather discredited that — is a result of twelve years of hard work and ceaseless study." Greene sat in his kite-like airplane around 1911 at an unknown location. Notice the sailcloth joining together the two wing tips of the fragile plane.
From the Rochester Public Library

The Municipal Airfield on Scottsville road (also called Britton Field) opened in 1918 years after pilots were landing in Genesee Valley Park, then called South Park. In this 1928 photograph, a second runway is being built and paved with crushed stone to accommodate the seven-city mail route set up in 1926 by Henry Ford.
From the Rochester Public Library

Capt. John Frisbee, a stunt flyer, in his biplane in 1911. This close-up shows the fragile homemade construction of his biplane. The steering column which appears to be bamboo is held to the wheel by a single screw. Thin wires seeming to stretch everywhere, and are held by small eyescrews to thin wood. In some places electrical tape holds wires and frame together.
From the Rochester Public Library

112

Evan J. Parker, a local pioneer aviator, standing inside the rigging of his dirigible in this undated photograph. Notice the fragile-looking wheel and the balast bags.
From the Rochester Public Library

The Rieflin Biplane, built by G. J. Rieflin and sons and flown by Fred Eells of Rochester, was one of the earliest airplanes in the city.
From the Rochester Public Library

113

Air shows in Rochester attracted a large crowd in 1934.
From the Rochester Public Library

The flyers from the Rochester Flying Service pose for this photograph near one of their airplanes. Notice the teeth painted on the propeller behind them. Air service revolutionized delivery and mail. The flyers are, left to right, standing: M. S. Burns, Bill Dunlop, E. G. Delano, Mac Dunlop, and W. E. Hutching, and kneeling; Vic Evans, Fred Haidt, and Guy Stratton.
From the Rochester Public Library

Lincoln Beachy flew the first bags of U.S. mail from Crittendon Park to South Park (Genesee Valley Park). He flew this plane on October 21, 1911. He steered the plane by leaning into a turn, then pulling on shoulder straps and using the wheel to climb or descend. He controlled air speed with foot pedals.
From the Rochester Public Library

With little boys leaping and young girls running behind, John J. Frisbee successfully flew the first heavier-than-air machine over Rochester on July 7, 1911, just eight years after the Wright brothers flew over Kitty Hawk. Frisbee smashed his light biplane into the trees at South Park (Genesee Valley Park) two months later.
From the Rochester Public Library

John F. Cooley brought his airship to South Park (Genesee Valley Park) near the Genesee River in 1911. He worked for twelve years to perfect this cigar-shaped "airship." It was one hundred feet long with an eight-foot crossbeam. Its four sails, arranged in pairs, lifted the ship with four thousand square feet of light sailcloth. It could carry three people. Cooley successfully tested his airship in July of 1895 in his hometown of Hornellsville. The electric airship could reach one thousand feet and could descend with the sails acting as a parachute. Unlike some inventions of the day, the pilot could steer Cooley's ship.
From the Rochester Public Library

A stagecoach moves into the Four Corners just ahead of a bicyclist in the 1890s. A horse-drawn streetcar draws through the sunlight, rushing the pedestrians in the crosswalk.
From the Rochester Public Library

The "Swedish Nightingale," Jenny Lind, sang at Corinthian Hall July 22 to 24, 1851, just three years after the hall opened. She remarked that Corinthian Hall had the best acoustics of any hall in the country.
Song sheet cover from the Rochester Public Library

The first of Edison's moving pictures was projected with an Edison Kinematograph in 1896 in the Lyceum Theatre. This photograph was taken around Christmas 1930. The bright lights of the theatres were supposed to give a Broadway atmosphere.
From the Charles Zoller Collection at the International Museum of Photography at the George Eastman House

Uncle Tom's Cabin *played in Rochester at Corinthian Hall on July 3 and 4, 1853. Broadside from the County Historian's Office*

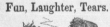

The Fox sisters, left to right, are Margaretta, Catherine, and Leah (Fox) Fish, who first demonstrated their power to communicate with the dead at a public demonstration at Corinthian Hall in 1849. Many prominent people joined this Spiritualist Movement. In nearby Hydesville, the sisters declared that they had made contact with the spirit world through "rappings." Their demonstrations became known as "Rochester Rappings." This attempt to communicate with the dead became the foundation of modern Spiritualism. An obelisk at Troup and Plymouth today marks the birthplace of the Spiritualist Movement.
From the Rochester Public Library

As a child, Anne Schieman visited the graveside of her grandmother in the 1930s. Throughout the history of Mt. Hope Cemetery, people have visited to remember loved ones as well as to view the natural beauty and monuments.
Courtesy of Ann Bidwell

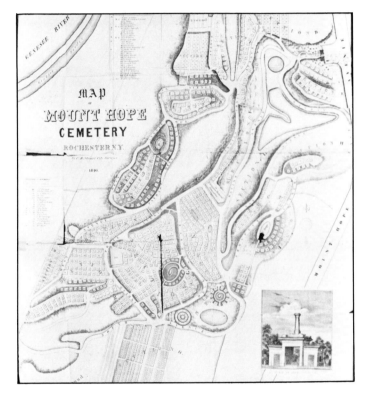

An 1846 map of the Mount Hope Cemetery drawn by City Surveyor C. B. Stuart. The drawing in the lower right corner is the view of the entrance gate.
From the Rochester Public Library

Mt. Hope Cemetery was the first planned municipal cemetery. It opened in 1838. A streetcar brought visitors to the cemetery, especially on Sundays. Families strolled through the hills and picnicked near their family's graves. Ellwanger and Barry Nursery donated fifty trees to the cemetery and encouraged cemetery visitors to stroll through their nursery and gardens located near the cemetery near the present site of Highland Park.
From W. H. McIntosh's History of Monroe County, at the Rochester Public Library

This engraving of Rochester about 1849, shows a beautiful city grown from a wilderness settled only thirty-eight years earlier. Viewed from Mount Hope, the road is visible on the right coming off of the bridge. A packet boat on the Canal is visible across the Genesee River. On the river canoeists race one another under the bridge past a pair of canoeists and a sailboat. A train steams by across the river, while a man fishes in the foreground on the canal feeder. Church steeples pop up all over the city. What a pleasant sight to the many pioneers who helped to settle Rochester and lived to see it grow to become the economic center of the Genesse country.

From the Rochester Public Library engraving by Flech, based on a similar drawing by E. Whitefield in 1849

The statue of Frederick Douglass overlooking the Highland Bowl at the Highland Park where concerts are held every year. Douglass' home was within the present borders of the park. The statue was originally placed on St. Paul Street, but was moved when traffic became too heavy. Douglass was a much admired man in his own time. A popular abolitionist speaker, he was in Boston at Faneuil hall when the news that Richmond fell to the Union Army arrived. Several people gave speeches when the audience began to call for Douglass to speak. John DeVoy reported in his History of Rochester, published by the Post Express, that the call "was caught up and repeated until it became a roar, and Douglass was finally carried to the platform on the shoulders of men who made their way through the dense crowd with difficulty. As he mounted the platform the applause became deafening. Hats, handkerchiefs, and even umbrellas and canes were thrown in the air, and it was some time before he could speak at all. Douglass' opinion was respected and sought after.

From the Rochester Public Library

120

Buffalo Bill Cody moved his wife and three children into a home on Exchange Street about 1874. He played in the old Grand Opera House in 1875. About a year later, the family moved to New York Street (now York Street). After about three years in Rochester, the family moved back to Nebraska, but daughter Arta remained as a student in Livingston Park Seminary in the old Third Ward. She was buried with the other Cody children at Mount Hope Cemetery in 1904.
From the Rochester Public Library

Buffalo Bill Cody's son, Kit Carson Cody, attended No. 2 School headed by Susan B. Anthony's sister, Mary. He died of scarlet fever in April, 1876. He was buried at Mount Hope Cemetery. In 1883, his sister Orra was buried at his side and in 1904 his oldest sister Arta was buried nearby. Johnny Baker, Wild Bill's adopted son, was brought to Mount Hope Cemetery in 1931, where his widow spread his ashes. Mary and Susan B. Anthony are also buried at Mount Hope Cemetery.
From the Rochester Public Library

The chapel at Mount Hope Cemetery. The Victorian fountain in the foreground was recently restored. The cemetery is maintained by the Rochester Parks Department and much of the restoration is done by the Friends of Mount Hope Cemetery. It opened in 1838. Family and friends later in the century spent many Sunday afternoons walking among the many flowers, trees, and magnificent monuments. A streetcar carried people out Mount Hope Avenue to the cemetery, where many stopped to visit the nearby Ellwanger and Barry Nursery. The natural beauty of the hills and valleys was created by the glaciers. An Indian trail intersecting the cemetery has been paved as a road. Postcard from the Rochester Public Library

Driving Park Bridge at the Lower Falls at the turn of the century showing the incline railway similar to the one built when Carthage was a thriving village here. From the Zoller Collection at the International Museum of Photography at George Eastman House

The parks in Rochester were once patrolled by mounted policemen. This policeman is patrolling Genesee Valley Park. Notice the PP for Park Police on the horse blanket and the braided whip in the policeman's hand. His uniform is formal and the helmet is soft.
From the Union and Advertiser, at the Rochester Public Library

Canoeing at the Genesee Valley Park is a favorite activity for park visitors.
From the Rochester Public Library

Skating on the Genesee River or the Erie Canal was a popular amusement in the last century.
Painting, 1862, from Rochester Historical Society Collection at the Rochester Public Library

An Abraham Lincoln character at Washington Square Park posed for Charles Zoller's camera at the turn of the century near the monument to Soldiers and Sailors atop of which stands a statue of Lincoln. The park was originally a courthouse square set aside by Elisha Johnson on his tract on the east side of the river.

When the tract was annexed to the west side Rochesterville, the courthouse square became a public square. It was the site of many patriotic gatherings.
From the Zoller Collection at the International Museum of Photography at George Eastman House

Elephants were often the main attraction at a circus. These elephants were probably from a visiting Ringling Brothers, Barnum and Bailey Circus. Often circuses performed at Falls Field but Barnum was so large the fairgrounds on the outskirts of the city were used.
From the Zoller Collection at the International Museum of Photography at George Eastman House

Sometimes performers attracted crowds at Sea Breeze. This may be Achille Philion who entertained crowds with his balancing act, walking on a ball down a spiral. He worked alone before joining Ringling Brothers, Barnum and Bailey Circus.
From the Zoller Collection at the International Museum of Photography at George Eastman House

These swan boats carried visitors over Trout Lake at Seneca Park for years before ending their season in 1922. A driver sat in the rear between the swan cutouts and pedaled the pontooned boat using a bicycle-like mechanism, while passengers sat on park benches. The poles sometimes supported a canopy.
From the Rochester Public Library

Seneca Park along the Genesee River at Brewer's Dock. The nearly still water offered a fording place to the Senecas who hunted and fished in the Rochester area. The natural beauty is preserved in this postcard from the St. John Fisher College library.

Maypole dances were popular among schoolchildren at the turn of the century. The parks were popular places for school and public events. Children in this postcard do a "May Pole Dance" in Seneca Park.
Postcard from the Rochester Public Library

126

This playground at the Baden Street Settlement House provided the neighborhood children with one of the few safe places to play. At the turn of the century, civic leaders pushed for more playgrounds, recreational areas, and parks.
From the Office of the City Historian

Seneca Indians returned to Maplewood Park every spring for the Annual Indian Festival. Indians danced, played music, and demonstrated their skills with a bow and arrow and a lance.
Postcard from the Rochester Public Library

The ruins of the Glen House after it was destroyed by fire. The elevator to Maplewood Park above still stands in this photograph. Through the arch of the Driving Park bridge, the powerful Lower Falls and the factories it drives are visible. From the Rochester Public Library

St. Joseph's Church on Franklin Street was destroyed by fire in 1975. Today the front of the building is preserved as an entrance to the St. Joseph's Park.
From the Charles Zoller Collection at the International Museum of Photography at George Eastman House

The purchase of horses to pull the hose carts and engines was a welcomed improvement in firefighting. Horses were paraded through the streets on inspection days and special occasions. They became mascots in the firehouses because the men depended upon them for speed. Many firefighters were saddened when it was decided to replace the horses with motorized fire engines in 1927 after most of the horses were disabled by a crippling hoof disease. Firefighters were aided by the purchase of fire engines and a ladder apparatus. In 1829, when the new equipment was purchased in Auburn, the inefficient bucket brigades ended. By 1832, Selye Fire Engine Company on Brown's Race was manufacturing fire engines. Rochester was equipped with six fire engines and a ladder apparatus. Volunteer companies raced one another to the fires, pulling their hose carts through the streets and sometimes on the board sidewalks if the streets were too muddy. In the winter of 1834, all the wooden buildings that were built out over the Main Street Bridge were destroyed when it caught fire. The public market at the end of the bridge was destroyed as well and had to be rebuilt. This unidentified steamer engine is displayed on a city street in the late nineteenth century.
From the Rochester Public Library

Lack of an adequate water supply was one of the most serious problems faced by firefighters. Until the 1930s, firefighters were summoned by ringing bells to form bucket brigades to fight a fire that at best could only be kept from spreading. People living in the countryside had to run into the village and ring the bells of St. Joseph's or Sts. Peter and Paul churches. Reservoirs buried at street corners supplied some water, but the amounts were limited by the dependence on rainwater to keep the reservoirs filled. Sometimes hollowed logs carried water from raceways, the canal, streams, or the river, but a dried-up or frozen water supply prevented firefighters from even containing a fire. Only a change in wind direction saved a favorite tavern, the Mansion House, from destruction in 1831 when firefighters exhausted the water supply on the burning frame buildings north of it. There were seven fires that year and sixteen the following year. Ordinances forbade the construction of wooden buildings, but those already built continued to threaten the growing city. Fires threatened buildings and lives throughout the century and the increasing number of multi-story buildings presented a particular problem to firefighters with inadequate water pressure. When a high pressure water system was proposed, Daniel Powers led the opposition, resisting a certain rise in taxes. He believed his new castiron building at the Four Corners was safe from fire; but when similar buildings were destroyed in the great Chicago fire, Powers quickly urged the construction of the Holley System that brought high pressure water for firefighting to the city and on February 18, 1874, the Rochester Water Works tested the pressure of their firefighting water supply near Powers' building. A five inch vertical stream of water shot 285 feet into the air making an impressive display to onlookers.
From the Rochester Public Library

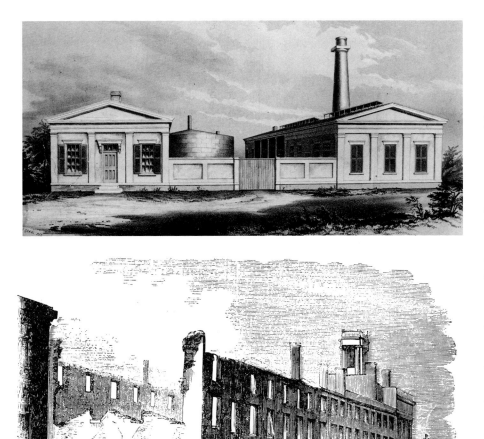

The Rochester Gas Works, built in 1848, began by serving homes and factories located near their works on the west side of the Main Falls. One of the worst disasters in the city occurred on December 21, 1887, when the Vacuum Oil Works sent fifteen thousand gallons of naptha to the Municipal Gas Works on Canal Street between West Avenue and the Erie Canal. The naptha escaped into a trunk sewer running parallel to the Western New York and Pennsylvania Railroad through Platt and Mill streets. A spark in one of the factories on Platt Street between Mill and State streets ignited the gas and for two hours there were explosions from the foot of Factory Street for two miles along the sewer lines. Eyewitnesses hearing the explosions, reported seeing manhole covers blown a hundred feet at every intersection along the sewer line. Jefferson Mills blew up and the Washington and Clinton Mills burned. Three men were killed and two others died of injuries. Women and children were also injured.
From the Rochester Public Library

Four domestics, three women and a boy, lost their lives in the fire that destroyed the Rochester House in May, 1853. There were about 120 people inside the hotel. Families boarding in this temperance house were forced to flee the flames when a fire began in the cooking and drying room. the Illustrated News, a New York City newspaper, reported " . . . the scene and dismay which occurred is inconceivable. Nothing remained of those who perished but a few charred bones, sufficient to enable the surgeon to designate them." Early firemen were helpless to extinguish fires quickly. City ordinances forbade the construction of wooden structures in designated parts of the city. The Rochester House, on the west end of the aqueduct at the corner of Exchange Street, was built from stone.
From the Rochester Public Library

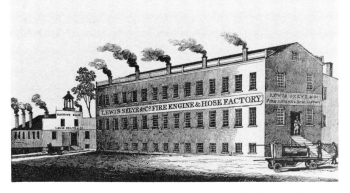

Drawing of the Selye Fire Engine Factory on Brown's Race from Sketches of Rochester by Henry O'Reilly, 1838.

Rochester House as it appeared before the fire.
From the Office of the City Historian

One of the Rochester Fire Department steam pumpers was captured by the camera of Charles Zoller as it passed in front of his house. Horse-drawn fire equipment was discontinued in 1927 after a deadly hoof disease disabled the horses. They were replaced by gasoline driven engines. From the Zoller Collection at the International Museum of Photography at George Eastman House

Fire horses, well groomed and ready for a call, are proudly displayed in front of an unidentified firehouse. The last fire call was answered by horses in 1927, before the horses were retired to the Monroe County Poor Farm. From the Rochester Public Library

Polished engines and pumpers, fully uniformed firefighters, and well-groomed firehorses parade through the streets of Rochester on Inspection Day in 1904.

Flags hang from several buildings where people can be seen leaning out of windows for a better view.
From the Rochester Public Library

A demonstration of fire equipment and technique. Firemen with buckets and swabs on the roof stand ready to work with firefighters on the ladders. On the street, buckets, ladders, and steam pumper stand ready for a real fire. when multi-story buildings were built too high even for these extension ladders, fire-fighters became concerned about water pressure and their ability to reach the upper stories.
From the Rochester Public Library

St. Joseph's Catholic Church at Ely and Minerva streets was torn down in 1926 to make room for George B. Hart's florist shop. The pioneer church was being used as a livery stable and carpenter shop when this photograph was taken in 1895. Firefighters were alerted to fires in the countryside by people who rang the bell of either St. Joseph's Church or Sts. Peter and Paul Church.
From the Rochester Public Library

An unidentified fireman poses in a pho-tographer's studio wearing the uniform of Engine Company No. 2, with the number standing out boldly on his belt buckle and chest badge. His hat on the chair displays a number two. He holds the trumpet in his hand. Volunteers were proud to be firemen. It was an opportunity to show bravery, save lives and property, and to socialize with other men. This photograph was tinted to make his shirt red.
From the Rochester Public Library; donated by J. P. Kislingbury

Icicles hang from the Granite Building after a fire destroyed the Sibley, Lindsey and Curr Dry Goods Store on February 26, 1904. This fire is still cited as one of

the most disastrous fires in the city's recent history.
From the Rochester Historical Society and the Rochester Public Library

Chapter Seven

"Remember your first thrill of American Liberty?" asks one
Liberty Bond poster. "Women! Help America's sons win the war,"
called another. "Our Daddy is fighting at the front for **you** —
back him up." Uncle Sam and President Wilson pleaded with the
American people not to conserve their dollars when buying
bonds. Immigrants, women, and lovers of children were called
upon to do their part. These posters campaigned for the sale of
Liberty Bonds in the second year of war in 1917.
From the Rochester Public Library

MEETING THE CHALLENGES OF A NEW CENTURY

WORLD WAR I

The war in Europe seemed distant to most Rochesterians, except for those whose hearts were still attached to their homeland. French, Belgian, Swiss, Dutch, German, Italian, and Austrian immigrants followed the war and organized to send goods and financial support to their countrymen. Eleven hundred Belgians left Rochester to join in the fight. French, Swiss, and Dutch soldiers left the city in small numbers to join them.

Despite rising prices, shortages, and dried up markets, Rochesterians might not have taken an active interest in the war had not the Germans sunk the *Lusitania* on May 7, 1915. A few vacationing Rochesterians were on board and survived the sinking that took 1,198 lives. Anti-German sentiment solidified in the community. Continued attacks on U.S. ships were viewed by Rochesterians as a call to arms and in light of German atrocities and enslavement of Belgians by Germans, Rochesterians were quick to accept the challenge.

A draft was begun soon after President Wilson's declaration of war. Though sentiment was strong against Germany, enlistments were slow. Even before the draft, Rochester men had joined Canadians, English, Polish, Italians, and French in the war. Divisions of the Naval Militia, Company H of the New York State Cavalry and the Third New York Infantry were the first to leave for active service. On September 7, 1917, forty-eight men boarded cars, and escorted by a band, they drove from the armory to the Lehigh Valley Station. Friends and relatives gathered at the stations each time a group of soldiers left for camp. The draft, more equitable than the one remembered during the Civil War, insured that men from all classes joined the active service.

One writer described Rochester's new soldiers as "all sorts . . . . They were boys who had watched with fascination the raising of lift bridges on the canal, who had risked their necks on the forbidden 'Indian Trails' along the river gorge, who had known the hustle of Main Street on Saturday evening, and the calm of Sunday morning."

The kick-off of the War Chest campaign informed citizens that "It is not necessary that every man fight at the front . . . . it is necessary that everyone who does not fight at the front, fight here at home. He must fight by working for victory, by sacrifice every day until victory comes." Many who could not join the active soldiers joined the Home Defense League to provide civil defense against sabotage. Others joined the Red Cross, swelling its rolls to over one hundred thousand.

Five thousand men and women were active rolling dressings, knitting clothes, raising money and supplies, and serving the canteen. Red Cross canteen workers met every troop train passing through the city. They not only offered a hot bath at the bathhouse near the New York Central Station, they also gave out meals, candy, postcards, and cigarettes. Fifty paid nurses were sent overseas and U.S. Army Base Hospital No. 19 was kept supplied with equipment, bandages, and trained nurses. Families of soldiers overseas were cared for.

The YWCA, the YMCA, the DAR (Daughters of the American Revolution), the K of C (Knights of Columbus), the Jewish Welfare Board, and many other organizations opened recreation centers, invited soldiers to dinner in private homes, and provided entertainment. Recreation centers were opened at Edgerton Park (then Exposition Park) and at Kodak Park where soldiers at the School of Aerial Photography could relax.

Besides the War Chest Campaign from which Red Cross funds were drawn, there were five Liberty Loan Campaigns. This combination fund drive included numerous charities under the name Rochester Patriotic and Community Fund, headed by George Eastman. It was the predecessor of the concept of United Way.

The shortages and soaring prices experienced early in the war only hinted at the conditions to come. Coal supplies, already short from the war effort, were further depleted by striking Pennsylvania miners. In 1917, homeowners could order coal in quarter-ton loads only. A few people hoarded supplies bought earlier, shortening supplies even more. Newcomers to the city were unable to buy fuel. Complaints were more numerous when newspapers pointed out the railroad cars of coal were waiting for shipment to Canada. The following year, needy families were supplied with coal by the police when their supply was gone. Although coal could now be bought in one-ton loads in 1918, the shortage was so critical that many public buildings were closed in January.

People learned to do without more than coal. They ate sugarless, eggless, wheatless, butterless, meatless meals. They planted Victory gardens all over the city and urged that the parks be plowed under. George Eastman joined in by planting his garden and lawn with vegetables, greatly annoying his gardener. German-Americans, struggling against anti-German sentiments, lived with the same shortages and worked equally hard in the city's factories.

About 60 percent of the manufactured products went to support the war. Eighty factories filled orders for clothes, food, equipment, and ammunition. Symington Company and General Railway Signal were making shells for England even before America declared war. Gleason Works made tools, gears, and castings, and made special screws for high explosive shells. Gleason also developed a method to lubricate the engines of submarine chasers. Stromberg Carlson supplied telephone and radio equipment. Rochester Gas and Electric Company recovered gallons of light oil derivatives

for high explosives and produced tar and ammonia. The Rochester Ordnance District produced 41,000 Lewis machine guns, 545,000 rifles, and twelve hundred 75 millimeter guns.

Increased production brought hundreds of workers to the city, creating a serious shortage of farm labor. The harvest years of 1917 and 1918 were so severe that vagrants were rounded up and put to work in lieu of jail. Blue collar and professional groups joined together to harvest crops.

The need for particular skills was met by the Mechanics Institute which trained women in mechanical drawing and optics. Following the war the Institute helped to retrain returning veterans. The University of Rochester put all of its energies into the war effort and about 250 of its students became active in the Students Army Training Corps in the fall of 1918. But the war ended before the Corps was able to put its training to work. Most women left their defense jobs and turned over the peacetime jobs to returning veterans.

The 1920s proved to be distressing when repeated strikes plagued industry, but it was not only in industry that there were changes. Society itself was becoming much more permissive, earning the decade the name the Roaring Twenties. One historian believed that the liberal behavior was caused largely by Prohibition which became effective in January of 1920.

THE RIGHT TO VOTE

"The secret to success is constancy to purpose," Susan B. Anthony once said. Certainly this was true for the woman's suffrage movement. The right to vote was won by women in 1918, but not one of the organizers of the woman's rights movement at Seneca Falls in 1848 lived to vote.

Like many other women, Anthony was also involved in the abolitionist movement and the temperance movement. She was a strong Quaker who became a Unitarian along with many other liberal minded Quakers. She was deeply involved in the temperance movement when she realized how few rights women had. She became a close worker with Elizabeth Cady Stanton who was one of the organizers of the Seneca Falls convention. Dr. William Channing, a Unitarian pastor, was an inspiration to her and other local suffragists like Rhoda DeGarmo, William and Mary Hallowell, Isaac and Amy Post, Samuel and Susan Porter, Frederick Douglass, Rev. Samuel May of Syracuse, Amelia Bloomer, and Ely Stanton, who met frequently to plan their campaigns.

Anthony attended the Woman's Rights Convention in Syracuse in 1852 and organized one in

A Thrift Kitchen run by the Monroe County Defense Committee on North Street advertised ways to conserve everything from potatoes to coal for the war effort.
From the Rochester Public Library

On September 6, 1917, Gov. Charles S. Whitman, Mayor Edgerton, and Draft Board members reviewed the first unit of the U.S. Army to leave Rochester from Edgerton Park. From there the troops left on trains for training camp.
From the Rochester Public Library

Many nurses and drivers left Rochester for the front. These three women served as nurses at Base Hospital No. 19.
From the Rochester Public Library

Rochester. She became a principal speaker and soon earned an international reputation as a womens' suffrage speaker, She remained a strong worker in the abolitionist and temperance movements also, and was instrumental in persuading the University of Rochester to admit women as students.

Rochester women were active in clubs and charitable causes. They were enlightened and had both the skill and the numbers to carry the suffrage movement. The energy of the women was often drained by causes such as war, epidemics, and urgent civic problems, but the dedication to the cause was persistent.

Anthony was seventy-one years old when she retired to her sister's home on Madison Street, but she frequently made trips to support woman's rights. She inspired a new, more numerous generation of dedicated women to take up the cause: women like Mary Gannett, Helen Montgomery, Mrs. Henry Danforth, Mrs. Max Landsberg, Mabel Clark, and Emma Sweet.

The women who marched in the city's first suffrage parade on Labor Day in 1915 were also the first women to appear as a marching unit in any local parade. Wearing yellow sashes across their white dresses and carrying banners, they marched as part of a statewide effort to win the right to vote in New York State. The right was not won that year, but a series of meetings and literature campaigns did win the vote in 1918.

With victory in hand, local organizers turned their attention to nationwide suffrage. That right was won only two years later with the passage of the Nineteenth Amendment making it seem an easy victory to younger women who had recently joined the campaign. But the movement that led to final victory actually began more than fifty years earlier. None of the original organizers lived to see victory, for the attitudes of many generations had to be shaped before the movement could be successful.

Anthony had marched and traveled hundreds of miles on speaking tours. She had been jailed for voting illegally. She was ridiculed by the press and the public for what some thought was a masculine manner and appearance. She had been with Frederick Douglass in 1859 in near riots like the abolitionist convention at Corinthian Hall. She saw the numbers of men and women involved in the movement swell, but she did not live to see the movement succeed in winning the right for women to vote in nationwide elections. Surely she had confidence that women would win the vote. She died in 1909 and was buried at Mount Hope Cemetery near her parents and sister. Their Madison Street home is a registered national landmark maintained by the Susan B. Anthony Memorial as a tribute to the memory of a great woman.

The Red Cross headquarters at Alexander Street and East Avenue was dedicated on May 8, 1918, with a flag-waving ceremony that brought patriotic salutes even from the young man on his tricycle.
From the Rochester Public Library

Red Cross workers at the Red Cross head-quarters on East Avenue and Alexander rolled bandages and collected other supplies needed at Base Hospital No. 19 during World War I.
From the Rochester Public Library

Every troop train that arrived in Rochester was met by Red Cross canteen workers who gave soldiers free cigarettes, chewing gum, candy bars, apples, and magazines. Soldiers were offered a hot bath at the bathhouse near the train station.
From the Rochester Public Library

Soldiers in training at Mechanics Institute (now the Rochester Institute of Technology) could find recreation and entertainment at the Hostess House at 32 South Washington Street.
From the Rochester Public Library

Food, especially grain products, had to be conserved for the Allies. Victory gardens were planted in backyards and vacant lots scattered throughout the city. Some people suggested the public parks be plowed under for planting. In this photograph, Alice B. Tough of Merchants Road stands in one of her five gardens.
From the Rochester Public Library

After the war, a troop train arrived in
Rochester carrying the bodies of soldiers
who died in service. People lined the
streets to pay their respects to the soldiers
as they marched solemnly to the Armory
on East Main Street.
From the Rochester Public Library

Inside the Armory soldiers stand guard
over their fallen comrades. Their solemn
expressions contrast with the excitement
many soldiers felt when they enlisted.
From the Rochester Public Library

Parades and speeches were held to sell Liberty Bonds. Bertha Pendento Eldridge was one of many speakers calling themselves "Four Minute Men." Many parades included artillery, marching soldiers, and attractions like the Liberty Coach.
From the Rochester Public Library

When the war ended, people drove their cars through the neighborhoods honking horns while men on running boards shouted, "The war is over!" Whole families hopped streetcars or rode a wagon or car downtown where Main Street around the Four Corners was crowded with as many as ten thousand people. Scores of people leaned out of windows or stood on balconies high above the street. The flag waving and patriotic costumes worn in the parade on the first Armistice Day on November 11, 1918, rivaled those of any Fourth of July celebration held in Rochester.
From the Rochester Public Library

When the war ended, friends and neighbors gathered for a celebration. Thousands gathered downtown while others drove through the neighborhoods shouting joyously, "the war is over!"
From the Rochester Public Library

Dressed in variations of American flags and waving flags wildly, Rochester people celebrated the end of the war on the nations' first Armistice Day on November 11, 1918.
From the Rochester Public Library

The tragedy of war remained in the lives of those who lived through it. A year after the war ended, mothers tended the graves of soldiers at Mount Hope Cemetery who died while in training in Rochester or who were taken from troop trains passing through the city.
From the Rochester Public Library

Susan B. Anthony worked with her biographer Ida Husted Harper in the attic of the Anthony home on Madison Street. Anthony died in 1909. Although not present at the first Woman's Rights Convention at Seneca Falls, she did attend the continuation of the meeting at Rochester.
From Ida Husted Harper's The Life and work of Susan B. Anthony, *in the Rochester Public Library*

Susan B. Anthony posed for this formal photograph near the end of her long career as an abolitionist and woman's rights speaker.
From the Rochester Public Library

Susan B. Anthony standing in the doorway of her home on Madison Street.
From the Rochester Public Library

Susan B. Anthony persuaded the president of University of Rochester, Rush Rhees, to admit women as students in 1900. She signed over her life insurance policy to help fund the program and obtained funds from other supporters. This class of women graduated from the University of Rochester in 1905.
From the Rochester Public Library

William Howard Taft came to Rochester
in August of 1911 for an encampment of
the Grand Army of the Republic (GAR).
Taft stands ready to address the crowd.
The former Civil War soldier standing
next to President Taft has lost his
right arm.
From the Rochester Public Library

Survivors of the Civil War appeared in
every major parade in the city and
crowds cheered them. The last local Civil
War survivor was James Hard who died
in 1953 at the age of 112. In this photograph the GAR (Grand Army of the
Republic) stands informally for an
unidentified parade.
*From a postcard at the St. John Fisher
College Library*

Civil War soldiers from Reynolds Battery gather around a cannon to prepare for Memorial Day observance near Washington Square. The trees, newly planted at the dedication of the Soldiers' and Sailors' Monument, are already grown in this photograph from the early 1900s.
From the Rochester Public Library

Frederick Douglass was honored on an unknown occasion by black Civil War veterans and an unidentified black woman at the former site of the Frederick Douglass monument that now stands at Highland Park.
From the Zoller Collection at the International Museum of Photography at George Eastman House

147

Hiram Edgerton (1847-1922) was a popular mayor, serving from 1908 to 1922. Under him, the Rochester Public Library was organized as well as a municipal museum. In this undated photograph late in his career, he stopped to pose before being driven away.
From the Rochester Public Library

Rochester in 1877 before the annexation of Charlotte under Mayor Hiram Edgerton.
Map from W. H. McIntosh's History of Monroe County, *1877*

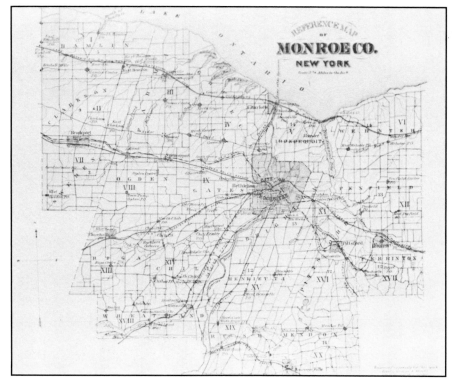

The camera of Charles Zoller captured a group of women gathered to sew American flags for an unknown occasion. Charles Zoller was an upholsterer whose avocation for photography became a profession. He photographed the gardens and homes of famous Rochesterians including George Eastman. He is credited with being the first photographer to bring the color autochrome process to America. The autochrome was a color process that created an impressionistic rather than defined image.
From the International Museum of Photography at George Eastman House

Ruth Muhlberger was photographed about 1921 peeking from inside a trunk in the yard.
Courtesy of Ann Bidwell

Frank Gannett (1876-1957), a temperance advocate, arrived in Rochester in 1918 and formed the Times-Union from the merger of the Union & Advertiser and the Evening Times. Gannett Newspapers is one of the largest newspaper chains in the country.
From the Rochester Public Library

Chapter Eight

In 1932, Gov. Franklin Roosevelt came to
Rochester to the Convention Hall off
Washington Square Park.
From the Rochester Public Library

ROCHESTER: FROM DEPRESSION TO WORLD WAR

THE GREAT DEPRESSION

When the stock market crashed in 1929, its relevance to the lives of Rochester's people was not readily apparent. But within months, thousands of workers were unemployed. People joined together to offer food, clothing, and money. Governmental and business budgets were cut and others were strained. The consumers' reluctance to make purchases sent production spiraling down and further deepened unemployment. Some men sold apples or pencils on street corners. Family meals became simple and soup kitchens were opened by churches. Families doubled up on housing to cut costs. Most people welcomed the opportunities for work and new construction as the city struggled to survive the greatest depression in the country's history.

In the depths of the Depression, the attention of Americans turned to Nazi Germany, fast pulling out of the Depression through the production of war materials. As the Nazis invaded one country after another, Americans finally realized that neutrality would not work. Rochester, along with other American cities accepted an increasing number of defense contracts. Unemployment not only became a problem of the past, but as men began to be drafted in 1940, factories were strained to find enough manpower to fill their increasing numbers of contracts. Rochester steeled itself to meet the challenge to survive the new threat—world war.

THE SECOND WORLD WAR

In the afternoon of December 7, 1941, the people of Rochester were startled by the news of the attack on Pearl Harbor and they feared for the lives of the Rochester soldiers stationed there. The Kramb family of Gates lost two sons serving on the USS *Arizona* and a third son died a few days later in the seas near the Philippines. Lt. Daniel McCann died in the attack on Pearl Harbor.

Within a week after the attack, Rochester experienced its first blackout. With London suffering almost daily bombardments, it was frightening to many Rochesterians to think about the safety of their own homes and families. Enemy aliens were questioned and forbidden to own radios. Many of these aliens were anxious to become citizens and their sons were in the U.S. armed forces. Japanese living in West Coast states were relocated and many came to Rochester.

Rochester soldiers stationed at Pearl Harbor during the attack wrote to their families about the attack. One wrote:

> We did see a bit of action the 7th, brought down a Jap practically in the front yard. I don't know the cause of his demise, but I like to think it was my Browning that did the trick. Anyhow, I threw about forty rounds at

him. About the maddest soldier I saw was _____, he emptied his rifle at the rising sun, couldn't find another clip so he bent down and threw a rock at them!

Craziest sight was two buck sergeants with two machine guns, flipping a coin to determine who could shoot first at an oncoming plane. Coolest soldier was a conscript holding down an automatic rifle with one hand and holding the Sunday morning funnies in the other. I sorta kinda thought that soldiers like these are gonna be rugged guys to beat. In fact I don't think they can be beaten, and that's something certain countries are getting wise to.

Another soldier wrote:

As you know, we had quite a time here on December 7th, and a great majority of us realized for the first time, just what "in the Army" means. I saw men who were so scared that they scarcely knew what they were doing, yet because of our army training, they retaliated to the best of their ability.

One boy, in particular, whom we had regarded as a softy, ran out to an airplane with an aerial machine gun and ammunition belt in his arms. Under a hail of enemy bullets, he set the gun up, and fired at the Jap planes with grim determination. He was sick with fear an hour after the "blitz," but during the few minutes of action we saw, he was right there, doing what we had been taught, plus some excellent shooting.

Although we did not have one anti-aircraft gun set up, and although none of our ships were able to get off the ground, Bellows Field is officially credited with five Jap planes. If we could accomplish that much damage under such circumstances as existed then, what amount of damage will we be able to do with the fighting force we have now? You can bet, it will be plenty!

The war was long and the costs to individuals at home and in the service was high. One soldier wrote home about the drudgery of war:

We have a very weak light for the room, but that is a luxury to us. It is the third night here and it is very peaceful after three weeks of sleeping through thunderous barrages . . . . We have been shot at with a wide variety of items (too wide a variety), but I still think the worst part of war is the dreary separation from loved ones, complete lack of creature comforts, fatigue, wet, cold, dirt!

Pick out the dirtiest job you know and do it for a month without bathing, going two or three days at a time without even washing your face and hands and you have a good idea of how war feels. If you can get good and wet and cold and stay that way, then you, as we say, "have had it." So spare a thought . . . . for the lads who make the communiques.

Another wrote of the high price of war:

Once out here we began to work immediately and have been in every carrier operation since. Some of them have been damned rough. I've lost some very good friends during these raids, and that, more than anything else has been my main dislike for this type of work.

Although the attack on Pearl Harbor came as a surprise, America's eventual involvement in the growing European war did not. Germany invaded Poland in September of 1939 and despite their sympathy for the Poles, most Rochesterians believed the United States should not intervene. Several months later, Germany invaded Norway and the heated debate between interventionists and isolationists grew hotter. When France fell in 1940, Hitler's intention to dominate Europe was unquestionable and the security of democratic countries was threatened. Still there were those who believed that until there was a continental attack on the United States, it should not intervene.

Because of their involvement in European war, when the Japanese attacked Pearl Harbor, Rochesterians were already prepared in Civil Defense, refugee relief, war production, and military preparedness. When the war came, the isolationists were silenced—left without a public ear. Plants stepped up production and unions pledged their support to the war effort. The numbers of defense contracts grew to a point that manpower became short. The city's high schools began to train their students to take jobs in defense industries under a program called VEND (Vocational Education for National Defense).

By 1940, a year before the war, fifty-five plants were filling one hundred million dollars' worth of defense contracts. The war demanded individual dedication that had not been called upon on such large scale since the Civil War. With the labor force siphoned off by the military, the industries accepting defense contracts were strained to meet their growing demands for skilled workers. The source from the city school district's VEND program was simply inadequate. Women with

*Eating a free dinner at the People's Res-
cue Mission during the Depression.
From the Rochester Public Library*

*Shoes had to last for money to buy new
ones was scarce. This man repaired his
own shoes at the people's Rescue Mission
during the Depression.
From the Rochester Public Library*

*A funeral inside the People's Rescue Mis-
sion about the turn of the century.
From the Rochester Public Library*

*Sometimes the only clothing men had
during the Depression was what they
were wearing. The People's Rescue
Mission kept a free laundry daily for men
to keep as clean as possible.
From the Rochester Public Library*

children, older men, and people of nationalities that were usually discriminated against in the workplace were now looked upon to fill the ranks of the labor force. Many plants were working three shifts, six days a week. In the year between September 1941 and September 1942, there were thirteen thousand more people employed in ninety-two city plants. Twelve thousand women registered for full-time work. Half of them required day care, so centers sprang up around the city.

The number of workers brought from the local labor pool of women, older men, and new graduates, helped to reduce the number of workers needed from outside of the area, but still the numbers that were attracted to Rochester by jobs put a new burden on housing. Vacant houses filled quickly so U.S. defense housing projects were built to reduce the housing shortage.

The labor shortage was felt outside the industrial plants. The migrant population was depleted by the military, so that there were labor shortages when harvest time came. The United States Employment Service struggled to meet the demand for harvest hands. Farm cadets were released from school and volunteers gave of their time. Together they contributed a significant amount of time. Private citizens planted victory gardens in yards and vacant lots throughout the city.

Despite the objections of many in the city, a Prisoner of War camp was located at Cobb's Hill from June to October of 1944. The prisoners worked in canning factories to help ease the labor shortage. They also cleared snow in the winter and performed various other tasks for which manpower was in short supply.

Not only was it a problem for farmers to get harvesters, but parts to repair their equipment were difficult to obtain and the gasoline rationing affected them as well as travelers.

Transportation became a growing problem as hundreds more workers commuted from the suburbs to work. Although nearly three quarters of the city's plant workers lived in the city, almost one third of them drove private cars. Only about 40 percent used the buses. It was not until gasoline rationing forced workers to leave their cars at home, that carpooling took root and bicycles again were numerous. Of all the inconveniences brought by the war, gasoline rationing drew the largest number of complaints. When the Japanese cut off the rubber supply and there were no tires for sale to the public that year, Rochesterians were introduced to the long years of rationing ahead.

Many people who were children during the war remember participating in the salvage drives which made a significant contribution to the war effort. In 1942 alone, the scrap metal collected was enough to build twenty-five light tanks. Hundreds of thousands of steel razor blades were collected by local barbers and hundreds of tons of rubber and industrial scrap. Many people remember walking the neighborhoods with wagons collecting salvage materials. The income generated by the salvage collections nearly carried the budget of the War Council. In 1943 the $140,000 budget was supported except for $3,157 and even less was in the balance in the years following.

Rochester's war bond campaigns were creative and gave new strength to citizens at home. There were events held to stimulate bond purchases. One popular attraction was a replica of the Liberty Bell that hung on a foot bridge built over Main Street. Bond buyers were privileged to ring it, reminding them and others what the bond drives were for. Rochester's citizens were enthusiastic. It was the first city to win the privilege to fly a Minute Man Flag over City Hall in recognition of 90 percent of its workers registering to buy bonds.

Throughout the war, Rochesterians continued the war relief efforts they had begun well before American involvement in the war. The British, Greeks, Chinese, Russians, Poles, Dutch, and Canadians were all sent relief from their sympathetic American countrymen. Clothing, shoes, money, anything that was needed was collected and sent. Even before America became militarily involved, the war was brought home to Rochesterians through their sympathies and involvement in other countries. As the Germans dropped bombs on Britain, Kodak brought the 156 children of its British workers to Rochester to find temporary homes.

Despite the reluctance of Rochesterians to become involved in the growing war, fifty-two thousand registered for the first draft in October of 1940, more than a year before war was declared. Draftees began to leave for training camps that month. The Naval Reserves and the National Guard were called into active service, but many, anxious to join in the battle, enlisted in the Royal Canadian Air Force and other foreign armies. Eleven hundred and thirty-nine died, over two thousand were wounded and over one hundred were missing or taken prisoner.

Hundreds of nurses from the five-county Rochester area became Red Cross nurses. Several area hospitals began to train them to meet the growing demands of the military. Over two hundred women in Monroe County joined the active service with the WACS, the WAVES, the SPARS (Womens Reserves in the Coast Guard) and the Marine Corps Womens Reserves. The Rochester Emergency Enlistment Forces (REEF) was organized to

Free milk was distributed to thirty-five hundred needy people in public and parochial schools from December 1935 to December 1936.
WPA photograph from the Monroe County Historian

The WPA provided jobs in clothing manufacture, quilting, building construction, and shoe repair. This shoe repair shop operated in Convention Hall during the Depression.
From the Monroe County Historian

Strikes in the clothing industry were frequent during the Depression. But the Bond Clothing Factory opened in 1934 on Hand Street and by 1935, it employed 1150 people to manufacture ten thousand pairs of pants a day. Modern machines sliced through twenty-four overcoats in a single cut. These clothing workers are sewing pants in May of 1935.
From the Rochester Public Library

stimulate enlistments in the area. It was so successful that it became a model for the nation in attracting women to active military service.

On April 12, 1945, Rochester mourned the death of Franklin Roosevelt. But Harry Truman soon gained the confidence of Americans and when Rochester received the news that Allied forces had landed in Europe there was hope that soon the war would end.

When news of victory in Europe reached Rochester, many people went to church to pray for the safety of their family and friends. Pfc August Corona and Helen Erie and her son, Leslie, are seen entering St. Luke's Church founded in 1817 by Col. Nathaniel Rochester.
From the Rochester Public Library

In 1932 "bonus marchers" gathered in the street to hear a speaker demanding veterans' bonuses and calling for a mass meeting of veterans at Washington Square.
From the Rochester Public Library

About 250 TERA (a pre-WPA state work relief program) workers shoveled snow from East Main Street near Front Street in 1935.
From the Rochester Public Library

Convention Hall off Washington Square Park where Gov. Franklin Roosevelt spoke in 1932 and where many other public

meetings were held. Today the building houses the GeVa Theatre.
From the Rochester Public Library

For several years throughout the 1930s, the American Communist Party celebrated May Day to support workers throughout the world. Sometimes joined by Socialist and Proletarian party members, the Communists paraded through the streets with signs that supported unions and protested WPA budget cuts, discrimination against the foreign born, and eviction of unemployed workers. On May 1, 1934, the Communist party gathered at Washington Square across the street from Convention Hall where they had met earlier.
From the Rochester Public Library

With so many men at war there were few hands at harvest time. In 1942, the Real Estate Board of Rochester pledged one day a week to harvesting crops for the duration of the season. The "Hands For Victory" campaign brought volunteers from a variety of professions. From left to right are: Austin Hale; Assemblyman Frank Sellmayer Jr.; James Killip; Follett Greeno; Curtis Glise; Frederick Schoeneman; Richard T. Evans; Lloyd Williams; Frank Bryant; John Tighe; and Henry Lyman. Greeno was the chairman of the Monroe County Hands For Victory campaign.
From the Rochester Public Library

Newspapers sold out quickly at Main and Clinton when early morning news of the Japanese surrender reached the streets on August 9, 1945.
From the Rochester Public Library

A Liberty Bell was hung from the center of the Liberty Bridge on Main Street. Bond buyers earned the privilege of ringing the Liberty Bell to call all citizens to support freedom.
From the Rochester Public Library

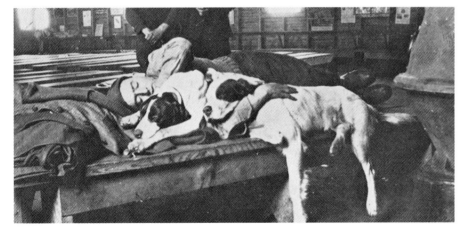

Red Cross nurses marched on Memorial Day in 1943. They are at the corner of East Main and Clinton.
From the Rochester Public Library

Soldiers trained hard at the Kodak Aerial School of Photography. In this undated photograph, an unidentified soldier slept on a hard bench by the pot-bellied stove with two exhausted canine companions.
From the Rochester Public Library

Patricia Hanna of Springwater drove a tractor down Main Street in Rochester in September 1944 to recruit tomato harvesters for farmers and canners. The Junior Chamber of Commerce Corps sponsored this "Help Harvest the Crops" exhibit.
From the Rochester Public Library

159

German and Italian POWs held at Cobb's Hill Camp were employed clearing snow or harvesting crops on farms around the city. These Italian POWs worked in the canning factories and fields. There were other POWs in Hamlin and Webster also.
From the Rochester Public Library

During War Week in June of 1942 church bells tolled throughout the city every day at 1:00 P.M. and the "Star Spangled Banner" played from loudspeakers strung along Main Street. James Farasey, Joe Hauser, and Sgt. John Evans (left to right) saluted the anthem. Joe Hauser expressed the deep solemnity felt during the early years of the war.
From the Rochester Public Library

On May 18, 1942, Consolidated Machine Tool Company was presented with the All Navy E. (for Excellence) Burgee pennant by Navy Lt. Comdr. John Tuthill, Jr. The Navy E. pennant was presented to manufacturers of defense materials who met or exceeded their quotas.
From the Rochester Public Library

In September of 1945 the campaign signs for the seventh war loan drive were removed from the East Main Street kiosk and replaced with a drive poster to raise money for the new War Memorial.
From the Rochester Public Library

Chapter Nine

Rochester and Buffalo still compete for the story of the worst snowstorm in memory. Though the snow can be hazardous and often inconvenient for travelers, the beauty is undeniable. This heavy snowfall greeted morning travelers in November 1953. Cars in this photograph were buried under the snow on Fitzhugh Street and a woman had to walk on the street through the tracks of cars.
From the Rochester Public Library

URBAN RENEWAL AND THE GROWTH OF A PEACETIME CITY

After years of rationing and sacrifice, people were looking forward to the end of the war. Although they quickly turned their attention to private affairs, the resettlement of refugees from war-torn Europe and renewed war in Korea kept Rochesterians ever mindful of war and the awsome power of the new atomic bomb.

Twenty thousand men and women from Monroe County were in the armed forces during the Korean conflict. By the end of 1950, 450 were in combat. The county lost 176 soldiers by the war's end. Still reeling from the reports of damage done in Japan by the atomic bomb, Civil Defense planned evacuation routes, emergency communications operations, and held "duck and cover" exercises in schools.

Returning World War II soldiers, thirty thousand strong by mid-1945, came home to a strong postwar economy. Many major industries like Kodak and Bausch and Lomb had developed international contacts during the war and they continued to expand. With the development of the Xerox machine, Haloid Company grew rapidly, expanding to Webster. Several city factories filled military contracts during the Korean conflict.

Retooling for peacetime production was not the only problem faced by the Chamber of Commerce Council on Post War Problems. Following the war, the council continued efforts they began in 1942 to employ and house the returning veterans. Women in the production line stepped aside to provide the veterans with their former jobs. They made great advances during the war: they were employed in previously all-male jobs, they began to wear slacks in public, they rode bicycles to work and for the first time since the Civil War,

they had provided critical manpower and civic leadership on the home front for a living wage.

The postwar suburban expansion of industry helped to draw skilled workers from the city, increasing suburban population growth. Hundreds of the veterans attracted by jobs left their city homes and moved to Webster where Xerox built a new factory. In only a decade Xerox increased its employment ten fold.

THE MIGRATION TO THE SUBURBS

All over the North, the inner city was changing as the stable, skilled workers who moved to the suburbs were replaced by black, poorly educated, less skilled workers. Word of the strong economy in the northern industrial cities brought thousands of poor, rural people from the South in search of jobs. Many of the blacks who worked as summer migrant workers during the war, decided to stay in the city in neighborhoods that traditionally housed new immigrants. They moved to the third and seventh wards into the homes vacated by second and third generation immigrants and returning soldiers cashing in their G.I. home benefit on a new home in the suburbs. By 1970 the 1950 black population of 7,670 had grown to 50,000.

Spanish-speaking immigrants, too, arrived in Rochester in growing numbers. Their search for jobs was complicated by their inability to speak English fluently. These newcomers settled in the Brown Square, Lyell Avenue area, and on the eastside around Lewis and Ontario streets. Between 1952 and 1980 the population of the mostly Puerto Rican immigrants rose from two thousand to sixteen thousand.

With more people working in the suburbs and many having moved there, better transportation was needed. Hundreds of people traveled by private cars rather than subway or bus. The growing number of suburbanites, particularly, needed fast and convenient transportation. Ridership on the subway was down so much by 1955 that the subway was discontinued.

The completion of the eastern expressway (490), not only gave the city easy access to the New York State Thruway (90), it carried suburbanites quickly to and from work. Houses and industry grew up all along the route. Transportation was further improved by the county when it took over the municipal airport. A terminal building and a runway nearly one mile long were added.

City/county cooperation grew through the 1950s. Besides the transfer of the airport, several other city functions became county functions. The city and county health departments merged to become the Monroe County Health Department in 1958. The Pioneer Library System was organized in 1956 to serve a multi-county area in which town and branch libraries were organized. The far-reaching audiences of Rochester-based radio and television stations solidified Rochester's influence over the metropolitan area.

The outlying communities shared in the triumphs and tribulations of the Baltimore Orioles' minor league team, the Red Wings, bought by Rochester Community Baseball. Suburbanites took to their hearts the Rochester Americans (the Amerks) too. The Rochester Royals played basketball at Edgerton Park until 1956 when it moved to the Community War Memorial, but failed to draw the crowds.

The city and county parks continued to draw crowds for boating, camping, hiking, baseball, flower exhibits, and just plain solitude. The Seneca Park Zoo is a favorite attraction among visitors and residents. Lakefront, riverfront and canalside parks give public access to the water and remind Rochesterians of the continuing importance of the waterways to the waterpower city. The city has undertaken a plan to revitalize the parks system along the river and to make an historical attraction of the once thriving industrial, water-powered Brown's Race area.

CHANGING NEIGHBORHOODS

Caught up in their private lives, most Roches-

terians worked at secure jobs, educated their children and looked forward to buying a home. They didn't realize families new to the city were unable to find good paying jobs or adequate housing. Settlement house workers warned that there were serious problems in the black community that needed immediate attention. Most Rochesterians were celebrating the strong economy and did not realize the depth of the problems. The hundreds of new blacks who had come from the South, ill prepared for employment in a technical job market, made tremendous demands on housing, the job market, and public schools. Friction developed between longtime residents of the community and the new migrants. The needs of the neighborhoods changed and the programs of the settlement houses changed to meet them.

Delapidated houses were demolished to clear slums in the 1950s, but many houses were also destroyed to make way for the increasing traffic. Buildings were demolished between Cumberland Street, Hyde Park, Clinton Avenue, and Central Avenue. Buildings in the path of the Inner Loop were razed in the early 1960s and dozens of others were knocked down to make way for I-490. Altogether, more than four hundred commercial and residential buildings were demolished to accommodate modern travelers.

The recent influx of new residents increased the demand for housing despite the out-migration of thousands of former city residents. The Baden-Ormond Redevelopment Project provided badly needed housing in that neighborhood. A few years later, in 1961, 284 more units were built in Chatham Gardens. Urban renewal districts were designated in the seventh and third wards and elsewhere and hundreds of delapidated homes were torn down. Low income housing units replaced single family homes.

But the housing needs were not adequately met, the schools were swollen with educationally disadvantaged students, and unemployment became a serious problem. Despite the efforts to address the problems, the critics complained that it was too little, too late. Riots in the black neighborhoods broke out on a hot July night in 1964 when police, responding to a call from Mothers For a Better Community, tried to arrest a drunk at a street dance. Many buildings in the neighborhood were set on fire in the Joseph Avenue area. Similar riots broke out in other Northern cities, creating tension that lasted for years.

The influx of Spanish speaking people to the neighborhoods complicated the services of the settlement houses and further burdened already overcrowded neighborhoods. The construction of

Returning veterans created a housing shortage. This 1946 Lyell Avenue housing unit was one of twenty buildings converted from former military structures.
From the Rochester Public Library

On April 5, 1951, the Times-Union *superimposed an A-bomb explosion over downtown Rochester to demonstrate the effect the bomb would have on the city. Following World War II, people were in awe of the power of the bomb. Civil Defense practice was taken more seriously then than today. A generation of Americans grew up under the threat of the bomb. The newspaper caption read: "If the bomb were exploded at two thousand feet, nearly everyone caught unprotected in the open within a half mile radius of the explosion would be killed. A flash of light accompanies the initial blast. Seconds later, the radioactive gases and dust form the familiar mushroom-shaped cloud that disperses harmlessly upward." The public did not yet realize that the radioactive gases would be the cause of more damage than the initial blast they so much feared. The old City Hall Annex in the foreground, formerly the Kimball Tobacco Company, was torn down for the new War Memorial. Except for the Times Square Building, the Powers Block, old City Hall, the Lawyers' Cooperative Publishing Company, and the National Casket Company, most of the buildings in this photograph are gone.*
From the Rochester Public Library

Captioned "Friendly Neighbors" in the scrapbook of the Baden Street Settlement House, this photograph shows some of the people in the neighborhood at a summer get together in August 1955.
From the Baden Street Settlement House, Office of the City Historian

the 153 unit Los Flamboyares in 1974 was the first public housing unit in the country built by a Hispanic organization, the Ibero-American Action League.

The flight to the suburbs continued through the 1960s. Five new shopping centers that opened in the 1950s to supply the thousands of new residents, gave stiff competition to downtown stores. Downtown revitalization was triggered by Rochester's first indoor shopping mall opened in 1961. Midtown Plaza on Main Street. A parking ramp was built near Midtown and Broad Street was extended.

The Landmark Society of Western New York played a leading role in preserving buildings and neighborhoods during urban renewal. Preservation Districts were registered and a renewed interest in historic preservation and architecturally significant buildings was sparked. Some neighborhoods, particularly Corn Hill, were restored as people in the 1970s moved into the delapidated, but solid, old homes in the newly designated Third Ward Preservation District. Values increased and many blacks could no longer afford to stay in their homes. This gentrification was the result of the renewed appreciation of the old architecture of the old neighborhoods. Hundreds of former city residents returned from the suburbs to escape the commuter traffic, gasoline prices, and more expensive suburban living. The city offered residents culture, convenience, and homes with an architecture unaffordable today.

Probably the most dramatic project during urban renewal was the demolition of the stores on the Main Street Bridge. Ever since the bridge was built it was the busy connection between the east and west settlements and a prime location for businesses. As early as 1827, businesses began creeping out onto the bridge, anchoring their supports on its piers. The businesses built on both sides of the bridge became an eyesore. When they were torn down along with some buildings on Water Street, the river was opened to public view for the first time in a hundred years.

THE CITY DURING THE VIETNAM WAR

Most of the young men and women that went to Vietnam knew little about the war before they left. Most of them went out of a sense of duty. At home patriotic ceremonies were held on holidays to honor the names of the war dead that became more numerous as the years passed.

As veterans began to return, many told stories that changed the attitudes of many of the supporters of the war. One returning veteran explained, "I think it was my second tour that I realized we weren't getting anywhere after I was there two years."

When the North Vietnamese launched the Tet offensive in 1968, American generals called for more soldiers and an escalation of military offensives. Protests in the city became more frequent and older, more conservative people joined the ranks of the protesters. But not everyone was against the war. The Liberty Pole became a rallying place as it had been in past generations, for people for and against the war. Speeches were made at Washington Square Park, pray-ins were held at churches and marches sometimes resulted in angry confrontations with police, though there were no injuries.

Newspaper coverage also changed after the Tet offensive. More articles focused on the war rather than human interest stories on soldiers away from home. Letters to the editor and editorials were critical of weak negotiations and continued war. Several trips to Washington were organized to bring five hundred to one thousand Rochester area protesters for each march as clergymen joined in support of protesters.

Rochester was one of only three American cities to officially denounce the war in 1973. By the time the war ended on January 27 of that year, 311 Monroe County soldiers had died in Vietnam. Though there was celebration at the end of the hostilities, it was not the widespread celebration that followed many other American wars, for involvement in the war was limited. Church bells rang in the city and car horns beeped in the streets. Prayer services were held for POWs and MIAs. It was a long war—twelve years long, but it was over for all but the MIAs and POWs, more than nine of whom were from the Rochester area.

Two years after the American troops withdrew from Vietnam, South Vietnam was overrun. Many Vietnamese escaped and settled in Rochester. Many other Southeast Asians emigrated to Rochester later and are the most recent immigrants to the city.

Demolition work on the old Baden Street neighborhood began in the fall of 1950 to make way for the Baden-Ormond housing project. Adults watching the demolition are from left: Joseph Neal, Edward Perdue, Honora Miller, Irving Kriegsfield, Nellie Cieslik, Rose Altman, and James Benvenuto.
From the Rochester Public Library

FIGHT supporters march near Ford and Broad streets to demand education and community unity in the 1960s amid riots, protest, and demand for better housing and education for blacks.
From the Rochester Public Library

The aftermath of the riots that broke out in the near northeast and southwest districts of the city on Friday, July 24, 1964. Gangs roamed the streets all night. So deep was the frustration and anger within the black community that peace could not be restored on Saturday, even with 550 city, county, and state police; but finally on Sunday, the arrival of 1500 National Guardsmen restored peace. Store windows were broken, stores were looted, and the neighborhood streets were left littered. Scores were arrested and four were accidentally killed.
From the Rochester Public Library

National Guardsmen patrol the nearly empty streets of Rochester's northeast and southwest neighborhoods in 1964 in the aftermath of weekend rioting.
From the Rochester Public Library

A Vietnam War protestor posing as Death, stands on a downtown street to warn that "war is not healthy." His bomb carries a montage of pictures that make his point.
From Gannett Newspapers

Too young to participate in the Vietnam War, a young man leans on the rifle of a Civil War soldier at the base of the Monument to Soldiers and Sailors at Washington Square Park. The park was the frequent gathering place for protestors and supporters of the war. Several parades began and ended at the park.
From Gannett Newspapers

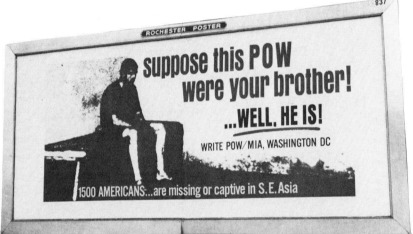

The Rochester Jaycees sponsored twenty-five billboards around the city in 1971 when there were nine Rochesterians in POW camps. This billboard on North Goodman Street was the first to be erected.
From Gannett Newspapers

In December of 1969, thousands of people marched in a candlelight procession down Main Street and East Avenue on their way to the Rochester Public Library for a rally. The candles were carried in memory of the war dead. The marchers chanted "Give Peace a Chance."
From Gannett Newspapers

Fresh beef on the hoof at the market on North Water Street is being walked through the street in this photograph from around the turn of the century. From the Rochester Public Library

A man making a purchase at the Public Market in 1949. The public market was so popular throughout Rochester's history, that when the old market burned down during the Main Street Bridge fire in 1834, merchants set up on the burned out lot until a new market was built. The Public Market, now on North Union Street, remains popular today. From the Rochester Public Library

Bicycling was a craze in the 1890s. There were bicycle clubs and planned trips along paths built from town to town. Bicycles were popular for travel to work also. Bicycles showed the variety of bicycles available in a Fourth of July parade in 1894. High wheel bicycles in the front are different from the standard touring bicycle shown behind them. The brick streets made it more difficult to maintain balance. From the Rochester Public Library

Roger Kline helped Frank Pillanora to mount an antique bicycle after he lost his balance in the Sesquicentennial parade in June 1984.
From the Rochester Public Library

Spectators sat on the water's edge to view the tall ships that arrived in July of 1984 to help celebrate the Sesquicentennial year. Tall ships used to come and go to Rochester's lake port and several Genesee River landings carrying cargo to and from Canada and ports beyond.
Photograph by Reed Hoffman; from the Rochester Public Library

In 1984 skeletons were discovered in Highland Park while landscaping was being done. When the first skeletons were discovered they were thought to be the bones of the Erastus Stanley family who had once owned the land; but after more than a dozen skeletons were excavated by the Rochester Museum and Science Center, researchers for the city realized that a little known cemetery used by the Monroe County Jail and Poor House in the nineteenth century had been uncovered. The bones were carefully removed from the exposed graves. The discovery added to the knowledge of the lives and treatment of the poor in the last century.
From Gannett Newspapers

The Red Wings Baseball Stadium in 1934.
From the Rochester Public Library

The 1939 Rochester Red Wings.
From the Rochester Public Library

This dramatic photograph shows the Commerce Building as it was blown up on November 8, 1980. Cheering crowds gathered to watch.
From Gannett Newspapers and the Rochester Public Library

Chapter
Ten

*The Strasenburgh Planetarium is part of
the Rochester Museum and Science Center on East Avenue.*
From the Rochester Public Library

FROM WATERPOWER TO BRAINPOWER

I t is significant that the first building on the present site of Rochester was an industry, that of Ebenezer (Indian) Allan, whose sawmills and gristmills were the first to harness the water power of the lower Genesee River two hundred years ago. From water power, through steam, electricity, and nuclear power, Rochester's industries have remained strong, building that strength on their versatility and diversity. From flour to flower, to shoes and clothing, to photography, Rochester has grown to become a major technologically-based community.

Industry met the demands of a changing world through the strengths of its people and the institutions they built. The first Yankee settlers, the Irish, Germans, Italians and more recently the Southeast Asians and Spanish speaking immigrants each brought with them skills needed by Rochester's industries.

The educational institutions include the University of Rochester, Rochester Institute of Technology, St. John Fisher, Nazareth, Roberts Wesleyan, SUNY at Brockport, SUNY at Empire, Colgate-Rochester Divinity School and Monroe Community College who educate students to follow professional careers in the community and the nation. Through such programs as Brainpower, industry continues to work closely with area schools, giving students an opportunity to be at the cutting edge of new technological advances.

Encouraged by a strong economic environment our cultural institutions have flourished. The Margaret Woodbury Strong Museum opened in 1982 and more recently the Memorial Art Gallery, The International Museum of Photography at George Eastman House and the Rochester Museum and Science Center, each have undergone major expansion.

Through cooperation between manufacturing and the community Rochester has become, as George Eastman once said, "A good place to raise a family."

The "Clock of the Nations" at Midtown Plaza Mall has been the meeting place for friends since the mall opened in the early 1960s. Every hour one of the twelve nations' cylinders opens a stage on which dolls from different countries dance to their native music. In a multi-ethnic city like Rochester, the twenty-eight-foot-high clock has a special significance.
From the Rochester Public Library

The Rochester Convention Center built during the Sesquicentennial year in 1984 adds to the modern beauty of downtown.
From the Rochester Public Library

The new wing of the Rochester Museum and Science Center.
Photograph from the Rochester Museum and Science Center

The Margaret Woodbury Strong Museum opened in 1982.
Photograph from the Bureau of Public Information

Fishing and hiking attract many visitors to the Lower Falls.
Photograph from the Bureau of Public Information

The Lamberton Conservatory in Highland Park.
Photograph from the Bureau of Public Information

The new addition to the Memorial Art Gallery links the main building to the Cutler Building.
Photograph by the City Historian

Boaters approaching the city from the river are rewarded with a spectacular view. The river has been opened to public view within the last two decades.
Photograph from the Bureau of Public Information

In May of 1989 President George Bush spoke at Eastman Kodak Company on his nationwide speaking tour for better education in America. Industrial Management Council's Brainpower Program, together with the Rochester City School's innovative teaching methods, promise a bright educational future for our area's students.
Photograph courtesy of Eastman Kodak Company

The interior of the new Bausch and Lomb research and development center is dominated by an atrium and skylit court.
Photograph courtesy of Bausch and Lomb

Introducing the Xerox 50 Series, named for the Fiftieth Anniversary of Xerography, a photographic process invented by Chester Carlson and now used in most offices.
Photograph courtesy of Xerox Corporation

Editing a manuscript in the Specialty Books Department at Lawyers Cooperative Publishing Company, a major book publisher.
Courtesy of Lawyers Cooperative Publishing Company

Delco Products Division, GMC, Rochester Operation Produces a variety of electrical components for the automotive industry.
Courtesy of Delco Products

The Rochester Historical Society has worked for decades to preserve and to collect Rochester's history for future generations. Their headquarters is at Woodside, the former Silas O. Smith house on East Avenue.
From the Rochester Public Library

The Genesee Crossroads Park (Major Charles Carroll Park) opened the river to view by visitors and workers downtown. The flags of the seven Sister Cities fly from the Y-shaped Sister City pedestrian bridge. The flags represent our twin cities in Bamako, Mali (Africa); Krakow, Poland; Rennes, France; Wurzburg, Germany; Caltanissetta, Italy; Rehovot, Israel; and Waterford, Ireland.
From the Rochester Public Library

The Genesee River looking south from the Upper Falls. The stores that were removed from the Main Street Bridge during Urban Renewal are still visible in the distance.
From the Rochester Public Library

One of many landmarks that binds us to the past is the Liberty Pole near the intersection of Main Street and East Avenue. The Liberty Pole was formerly a wooden pole that stood a century ago in 1889. Today the Liberty Pole is made of stainless steel.
From the Rochester Public Library

The statue of Mercury was carefully lowered by a crane as spectators gathered to see the large community landmark preserved for future use. The building was used as the City Hall Annex for years after the tobacco company left it. The statue was eventually placed on the top of the Lawyers' Cooperative Publishing Company across Broad Street from where it once towered over the city. It again serves as a guide to residents and an attraction on Rochester's skyline.
From the Rochester Public Library

The Kimball Tobacco Company building was torn down in 1952 to make way for the Community War Memorial, a center used for concerts, circuses, and other events. The project, painted on the side of a nearby building, shows the boundaries of the Memorial. The smokestack of the old tobacco company lifts the statue of Mercury high above the rubble.
From the Rochester Public Library

*Cutler Union, named for former mayor
James Cutler, was opened in 1933 as a
women's building on the old campus of
the University of Rochester on Prince
Street and University Avenue. It stands
today as part of the Memorial Art
Gallery.
From the Rochester Public Library*

BIBLIOGRAPHY

Newspapers

Anti-Masonic Enquirer
City Newspaper
Democrat & Chronicle
Liberal Advocate
Monroe Republican
Rochester Album
Rochester Daily Advertiser
Rochester Daily Democrat
Rochester Daily Union
Rochester Gem & Ladies' Amulet
Rochester Observer
Rochester Republican
Rochester Telegraph
Times Union
Union & Advertiser

Articles

Rochester History

Black, Sylvia and Harriett J. Naylor. "Rochester & World War I." October, 1943.
Lenti, Vincent. "A History of the Eastman Theatre." January, 1987.
Lutz, Alma. "Susan B. Anthony and John Brown." July, 1953.
McKelvey, Dr. Blake. "Colonel Nathaniel Rochester." January, 1962.
_____ . "Flour Milling in Rochester." July, 1971.
_____ . "The Germans in Rochester, Their Traditions and Contributions." January, 1958.
_____ . "Historical Aspects of the Phelps & Gorham Treaty of July 4-8, 1788." January, 1939.
_____ . "An Historical Review of the Italians in Rochester." October, 1960.
_____ . "A History of the Rochester Shoe Industry." April, 1953.
_____ . "Indian Allen's Mills." October, 1939.
_____ . "The Irish in Rochester, An Historical Retrospect." October, 1957.
_____ . "The Men's Clothing Industry in Rochester's History." July, 1960.
_____ . "Railroads in Rochester's History." October, 1968.
_____ . "Rochester and the Erie Canal." July and October, 1949.
_____ . "Rochester at the Turn of the Century." January, 1950.
_____ . "Rochester Learns to Play: 1850-1900." July, 1946.
_____ . "Rochester's First Year in the War for Survival." January, 1943.
_____ . "Rochester's Mid-Years: Center of Genesse Country Life 1834-1884." July, 1940.
_____ . "Rochester's Near Northeast." April, 1967.
_____ . "Women's Rights in Rochester: A Century of Progress." April and July, 1948.
Parks, Dan. "Cultivation of the Flower City." July and October, 1983.
Perkins, Dr. Dexter. "Rochester, One Hundred Years Ago." July, 1939.
Rochester GI's (edited by Dr. Blake McKelvey). "Life in the Armed Services." January, 1946.
Rosenberg-Naparsteck, Ruth. "A City in Conflict: Rochester During the Vietnam War." July and October, 1986.
_____ . "A Growing Agitation: Rochester Before, During and After the Civil War." January and April, 1984.
_____ . "A History of the Circus in Rochester." July, 1987.
_____ . "Life and Death in the 19th Century." January and April, 1983.
Van Deusen, Glyndon. "Thurlow Weed in Rochester." April, 1940.

Rochester Historical Society/Publication Fund Series

Bryan, Aaron. "King's or Hansford Landing." 14:167-174.
Dow, Harriet Brown. "Influence of Women in the Life of Rochester." 11:189-207.
Hatch, Jesse W. "Memories of Village Days—Rochester, 1822-1830." 4:235-247.
_____ . "The Old-Time Shoemaker and Shoemaking." 5:79-95.
Kosok, Paul. "Lewis Henry Morgan on the Flour Mills and Water Power at Rochester." 23:109-115.
McGregor, A. Laura. "The Early History of the Rochester Public Schools: 1813-1850." 17:37-73.
McKelvey, Dr. Blake. "Early Library Developments In and Around Rochester." 16:11-50.
_____ . "The Flower City: Center of Nurseries & Fruit Orchards." 18:121-169.
Marsh, Ruth. "A History of Rochester's Park in the Civil War." 22:4-76.
Morgan, Lewis Henry. "The Flour Mills, and Flour Manufacture of Rochester." 23:116-127.
Osgood, Harmond L. "Rochester—Its Founders and its Founding." 1:53-70.
Quarles, Benjamin. "Frederick Douglass and John Brown." 17:291-299.
Shafer, Hayward Mason. "Aviation in Rochester." 14:289-310.
Sheldon, George B., Jr. "The Expedition of the Marquis de Denonville against the Seneca Indians—1687." 4:1-82.
Turpin, Morley. "Ebenezer Allen in the Genesee." 11:313-338.

Books

Ackerman, Carl. *George Eastman.* Boston, 1930.
Art Work of Rochester. Rochester, New York: Parish Publishing Co., 1913.
City of Rochester, Illustrated. Rochester, New York: *Post Express* Printing Co., 1890.
Cross, Whitney. *The Burned-Over District.* Ithaca, 1950.
DeVoy, John. *A History of the City of Rochester.* Rochester, New York: *Post Express* Printing, 1895.
Homer, Harmond. *Monroe County: The Sesquicentennial Account of* the Local History Division, Rochester Public Library.
Lee, Florence. *Pleasant Valley: An Early History of Monroe County and Region 1650-1850.* New York, 1970.
McIntosh, W. H. *History of Monroe County, N.Y.* Rochester, New York: Everts, Emayn & Everts, 1877.
McKelvey, Dr. Blake. *Rochester: An Emerging Metropolis: 1925-1961.* Rochester, 1961.
_____ . *Rochester on the Genesee.* Syracuse, 1973.
_____ . *Rochester: The Flower City: 1855-1890.* Cambridge, 1949.
_____ . *Rochester: The Quest for Quality: 1890-1925.* Cambridge, 1956.
_____ . *Rochester, The Water Power City: 1812-1854.* Cambridge, 1945.
Mangione, Jerry. *Mount Allegro.* Cambridge, 1942.
O'Reilley, Henry. *Sketches of Rochester; With Incidental Notices of Western New York.* Rochester, New York, 1838.
Parker, Jane Marsh. *Rochester, A Story Historical.* Rochester, 1884.
Peck, William F. *Semicentennial History of the City of Rochester.* Syracuse, 1884.
Rochester, Illustrated. Rochester, New York: H. R. Page & Co., 1890.
Turner, Orsamus. *History of the Pioneer Settlement of Phelps & Gorham's Purchase.* Rochester, 1851.

INDEX

ABOUT THE AUTHOR

Ruth Rosenberg-Naparsteck is City Historian of Rochester, New York. She has edited the past six quarterly volumes of *Rochester History* and has published numerous articles in newspapers as a reporter and as a free lancer. She is the author of *A Portrait Of Lycoming County*, a history of Lycoming County, Pennsylvania, and is currently working on an illustrated history of the Genesee country for young people.

The author has excavated at archaeological sites in Muncy, Pennsylvania, and Beersheba, Israel. She holds an A.A. degree in journalism and mass communications from Point Park College, a B.A. in sociology and anthropology from Lycoming College, and an M.A. in American history from the State University of New York. She has taught college students and frequently lectures on local history.